EREBUS

JANE SUMMER

SIBLING RIVALRY PRESS
LITTLE ROCK, ARKANSAS
WWW.SIBLINGRIVALRYPRESS.COM

Sibling Rivalry Press, LLC
PO Box 26147
Little Rock, AR 72221
info@siblingrivalrypress.com

www.siblingrivalrypress.com

ISBN: 978-1-937420-90-1

Library of Congress Control Number: 2015930517

First Sibling Rivalry Press Edition, March 2015

for my great dogs,
      may they forgive me

            for Anya, who makes me hostage
                  to the world

NOTE TO THE READER

This story is based in fact. Every effort was made to adhere as close to actual events as possible. But it is above all a work of art, and thus a certain amount of leeway must be allowed for the distillation of information into that other ineffable thing that sustains the spirit.

"In [the 1500s] friendship was not, as it is among adults of our own time, simply one of the pleasures of social life; it was, as it still is today for the child and the adolescent, a lasting bond comparable to love, so strong that it sometimes even survived death."

Philippe Ariès, *The Hour of Our Death*

INTRODUCTION

During the late 1970s, the national carrier Air New Zealand offered regularly scheduled Antarctic sightseeing flights departing from Auckland and crossing over scenic locations on the polar continent. The nonstop roundtrip excursion took about 11 hours and cost what would be equivalent today to US $1,000.

On the morning of 28 November 1979, Air New Zealand flight TE901 took off at 8:21 am, with an ETA of 7:05 that evening. By 8:30 pm, the aircraft had not returned. Radio contact could not be raised. Operating initially on the theory that the flight had lost its way, airline executives soon were forced to accept that the aircraft had depleted its fuel reserves. A statement issued to the media set off a heart-sickening chain of events. Broadcasters interrupted regular programming to declare the plane officially "missing."

There were 257 people on board.

That evening the news riveted all of New Zealand and Australia. In that part of the world, the unfolding disaster would sear memories between generations the way the Kennedy assassination had across America.

While the vast majority of passengers and crew were New Zealanders, also on board were citizens from Australia, Canada, France, Japan, Switzerland, the United Kingdom, and the United States.

A friend of the author had been among the adventurers on flight TE901.

2013

WELCOME ABOARD

Planes crash.
Despite statistics

we're not
dummies.

Word Association

car	/	tire
boat	/	sail
train	/	conductor
plane	/	crash

Daughters of aviators
deeply pleasured with liftoff,

*To get a flying machine—
say the McDonnell-Douglas DC-10-40
with a maximum takeoff weight
of 565,000 pounds—
off the ground, force
must be created that equals
or exceeds the force of gravity.
This force is called lift.*

*Lift is created by the flow of air
over an airfoil (the plane's wing), shaped
to cause air to flow faster on top
than underneath. Fast flowing air
decreases pressure while slower moving
air increases pressure. This difference
in pressure surrounding the airfoil
results in lift.*

the body sinking
like an anodyne

into its foam
economy class seat,

even we
never take

safe landings
for granted.

A tail-gunner, my father
spent the war freezing

in his far compartment
and paltry electric

flight suit. My father made it through
the black carpet

of Luftwaffe skies,
the awful turbulence

of formation flight, deafening war
machines that diminished

his hearing.
In that distant

tail compartment
my father gunned

through combat
on his knees. Because

he survived I believe
it's my birthright

to fly. This I tell myself
when things get rough

at 30,000 feet,
the plane drops through

sinkhole upon sinkhole,
a devildog shakes us by the tail,

or those I love book
and board again, again

jetting into the blue
swimmerless seas.

I imagine my father's
Flying Fortress,

tail shot to shit, three engines down
over Germany,

and what must have overcome
his men in their shearling collars

when wheels found ground in East Anglia
and they called it home.

OUR FLIGHT TIME TODAY

Don't expect an elegy.
I'm unofficial, uninvited,

no spouse, certainly not
family if family means

a certain beauty and turned
foot. I've never wept

at the crash site nor signed
the book of mourning,

it wasn't me kneeling before
the frozen steel

cross, contemporary koru
sculpture, not me in prayer at the stained

glass memorials to well-known
unknown passengers.

I'm American and Erebus
anniversaries—one year,

ten, thirty—have passed by
where I live

> *10011*
> *10003*
> *10024*
> *10463*
> *11215*

with less notice
than we give the Queen's Birthday.

What a strange insult,
like the fourth of July in Auckland

without so much as a fizzle or spark.
My birthday's gone

unrecognized more than once
in foreign places.

Who's responsible and who's
to blame. A yankee, I've been

so out of it for so many years
I'm not even sure

if I lost Kay in that
crash or she lost me.

What I've come to say is all
that's left is her

absence, and it has been with me
like furniture in the dark

you're bound one night
to step into. Don't

expect an elegy
raising the dead, praising

the dead. Despite our best intentions,
we forget the dead.
Do they forget us?

It is winter in New York. I'm 58 and always
cold. I've never lived in a room

adequately heated. But as a child I was drawn
to the Poles, where the world begins

and ends. I built a sugar cube
igloo in grade school and when snowfall

forged the land anew
trekked my plastic blue

snowshoes on the tundra
of dreams—mush! mush!

To the high latitudes! To the world
as it really is, without interference

in asphalt, iron and grid. To rise above
the patchwork

which has such control over
our days—How could anyone refuse

flight
to Antarctica?

1990

SEAT BACKS IN THE UPRIGHT POSITION

I don't want to go
Down Under. My German

Shepherd is 14.
He won't last.

My editor says this
is the chance of a lifetime,

the dog's a bad excuse.
How much I love

seems of no consequence. Why would
I want a three-month junket

to Australia and New Zealand—
bush vigor, tainted colonialism?

I'm first to admit
I've no sense of adventure.

"Chance of a lifetime." Give it to
one of the junior editors, someone

who's never been west
of New Jersey.

"I'm offering it to you."
My dog won't write

or get on the phone
those overseas months. He will,

however, teeter on.
Until. And then.

My magnificent
German Shepherd

with the silver aegis
of fur. I'll never talk

of the guilt
for having left. Still

into my fifties I dream
I've committed irreversible

> *Make the worst of what you've done*
> *luminous*

sins and I never tell
anyone but the psychiatrist

though all she does
is listen. And listen,

I'm afraid, is all
I did for Kay.

How like Kay to have told this tale:

In the time of the dynasties, among two
devoted friends, one was a master of the lute,
one a keen listener.

After the lutenist would play The Mountain
Song, the listener friend remarked, "When you
play The Mountain Song, a snowy peak towers
before my eyes."

When lutenist played The River Song, the
listener exclaimed, "When you play The River
Song, I hear rippling water beside me."

News of the listener's sudden death reached his
friend. The lutenist held his instrument in his lap
and cut its strings.

My editor lays out the deal:
If I assist our Sydney office and produce

a travel column, the magazine covers
my full salary and expenses. If I cite

Air New Zealand as my carrier,
the airline comps my flight

round-trip. Is this how
the world works? (Thirty-six and still stupid.)

Somewhere closer to the equator
than I've ever been, a flight attendant hovers,

blanketing the body that has come this far
with me. More than halfway toward

sleep, I mistake her gesture
for love. O god of small animals,

it's me. I'm calling from this jumbo jet,
first class! Please

give my dog the scent of sun on the iron
gate at St. Mark's, deep sleep, days

without thunder. Say in his language
speaking through the unwashed

nightshirt left behind,
I am with him.

Don't   be   afraid   of

who   you   are

Make   the   worst

of   what   you've   done

luminous

Let   no   one   live

in   oblivion

What's that you say? Who's talking?
I can barely hear. Stratosphere

chatter must be at it. Was I dreaming?
Traveling in deep memory? I wonder.

I wonder if anyone down below
in Kiribati is thinking

about me. I'm thinking about them.
It's a new day.

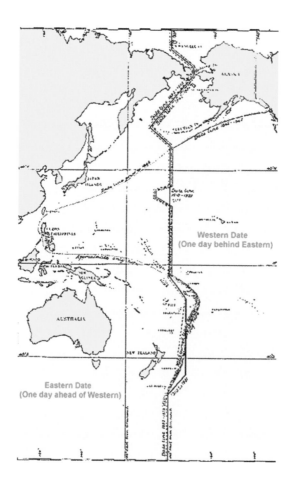

I'm in my Sydney hotel room—
spacious and bright, the five-star

deal, the ominous calm, a little death in every object
from side chair to sewing kit

and everything has its place, the world
well ordered

and custard yellow. Sydney, lush
Sydney, surprisingly sensual for an English

speaking city, a treasury of harbors and opals,
and lunatic kookaburras

too accurately predicting
rain, and when rain comes

unrelenting on Pitt Street, its little feet
stamping on my windows, I won't let it in.

One night in April while I'm glad to be lost
in the Ayers Rock-size bed, news of a friend

dying in a commercial jet
that slammed the Swiss Alps

jolts me awake. Finding calm
in the bedside lamp's bowl of light,

I detail the nightmare
on a Renaissance Ramada

notepad. If it's an omen
a fax must be sent. Posthaste.

My Sydneysider colleague takes the dream
to mean something's coming for me

"in the distant future, a great change."
Buttering her toast with Marmite,

she invites me to join her firewalk
after work. I prefer to eat sardines

in my hotel room and weigh
myself in stones.

How patient the dead. It will be thirteen
years before that leaf

of hotel notepaper slips
from a frayed notebook.

> *Awful dream: X dies in Alps crash*
> *+ I say maybe they'll find her*
> *preserved by the cold but everyone*
> *says I'm fooling myself + my loss*
> *feels inconsolable*

The unconscious crashing
into sleep with its parallels: snowy

mountain, dear friend flying off, the boom
bang of it—does significance

ring any louder?
Why

does it take decades
to wake and shake me?

We think we know
what we're fearful of forgetting—

—It's so much worse
than we ever imagined.

1979

FASTEN YOUR SEATBELT

Kay Barnick
   29 DOB: 5/3/1950 California SSN: XXX-XX-4799

Marion Barnick
   59 DOB: 10/11/1919 Idaho SSN: XXX-XX-9239

Not Jehovah's Witness nor a speaker
in tongues, not Mormon, Mennonite, Shaker

or Quaker. How often does Marion explain
what she is

and is not? Her sacred book proclaims, Death
is only the belief

in death. Please let me
join that church.

Long distance. Person to person.
Marion calls her

oldest daughter, uninterested
in accustoming herself to having an

only daughter. Where she's calling from
the backyard lemons gloat in the arms of the sun. *Let's go*

to Antarctica! In New York,
night's already come.

What makes Kay quail? She sits on her bed. She catches
her breath with a butterfly net. The pleasure

of traveling with Marion is not disputed. She remembers
India, remembers the local authorities refusing

her mother's students, all women,
permission to fly

outside the airport traffic pattern. Now
they can laugh, and Marion has since

brought so many students to the States, making sure
they put down in every muddy field and farm

until the women owned
the soft landing. No grudge, mother and daughter

hold India in the cup
of their hearts.

Tonight, it seems Antarctica's ventriloquist calls
from San Jose, *Let's go!* They can tag this

leg onto a larger journey
planned earlier,

the perfect finish
to their Milford Track hike.

> *Billed as the "finest walk in the world,"*
> *the Milford Track covers 33.2 miles of*
> *stunning New Zealand Fiordland, alpine*
> *passes, rainforest, lakes, waterfalls and*
> *glacially carved valleys.*

How do they imagine Antarctica? From New Zealand, the Pole's
eleven hours of luxury

flight. If Kay envisions void
and vacancy, Marion perceives the continent's untouched

topography, the presence of the divine.
Or maybe it's the idea

of Antarctica, something calling
to the adventurer

in Marion, who has campaigned the great world
by air, the choice mode of transportation for so many

gods. Besides, what explorer could resist the publicity
brochure trumpeting Sir Edmund Hillary

as their in-flight guide, though Kay might think him
a bit of the daredevil.

> *A speaking tour caused Sir Edmund Hillary*
> *to cancel his plans. Good friend*
> *and climbing companion Peter Mulgrew*
> *stepped in on the ill-fated flight.*

Does the dance of the emperor
and rockhopper penguins in their satiny

robber baron suits draw both women? Are they
lured by the pre-speech primordial

elephant seals, the sweet Weddell
and crabeater, whose quizzical eyes

hold an untellable history
of slaughter? Will they sight the killer

whale's startling breach? God knows what
animal life Marion and Kay might see!

Skua gulls—
the hyenas, the vultures
of the Pole—

Let's go to Antarctica! Crossing
the South Magnetic Pole, Marion

in the slender widebody, mirrors the heroic gesture
full of 19th-century inquiry. For Kay,

hedging in the East
Village, Antarctica whispers wasteland, white-washed

whalebone monuments to destruction
on fast ice, the heroic failure. *Let's go to Antarctica.*

The Ninety-Nines, those high-flying
gals, won't hesitate to sign on with Marion

for the jamboree, though at the last minute
their plans change. A woman calls her

oldest daughter, *Let's go to Antarctica.* An airline
promotes a complimentary Champagne Breakfast

with Lamb Kidneys, lunch of
Bay Prawns and Antarctic Scallops in an Icy Mint Sauce

and for dessert, Peach Erebus.
The flight will be unforgettable.

Erebus	*In Greek mythology, Ερεβος (Erebus), son of Chaos, personification of darkness; the first realm of the gloomy underworld through which all the dead must pass before reaching Hades*
Mount Erebus	*Southernmost volcano on Earth and second highest in Antarctica, on Ross Island; remains active*
Ross Island	*Formed by four volcanoes, including the now dormant Mount Terror*
	Southernmost entry point for many Heroic Age Antarctic expeditions; both Shackleton's and Scott's huts remain, preserved as historical landmarks; polar researchers make Scott Base (New Zealand) and McMurdo Station (US) home year round

FLOTATION DEVICE

She smiles at me.
So we begin. Who would not

return the stranger's
invitation?

In the newsroom
there's talk

of the heat
above and below,

the collapse of ice,
global instability,

the Western Antarctic
Ice Shelf shedding

city-sized bergs
to the seas. The rising

tide sends survivalists
for higher ground. This woman,

Kay Barnick, is higher
ground. I know it

right away.
Like I know

I'm sick
of all the lies I tell.

Like I know she will go
to Antarctica.

Who am I
to say stay?

I'm
two desks away.

You'll never amount to anything
unless you cut that hair of yours
sit up straight wear a little rouge
start dating men eat meat take
dance class quit smoking call your
father lose weight admit
sooner or later your dog is going to die get
contacts use
fewer adjectives

*Don't be afraid
of who you are*

she offers
then covers my untouchable hand

with her road-mapped hand
in the office

cafeteria. "Roxanne"
peals from the short order cook's radio

Put on the red light

and like a Nansen passport I am
recognized in a dozen languages.

I never give Kay much
more than raffia baskets

of chanterelles and apricots because
we have only just begun

but in this beginning
I might not be a girl

anymore but that fully grown
thing with wings.

> *And it is those who desire the good of their friends*
> *for their friends' sake that are most truly friends,*
> *because each one loves the other for what he is,*
> *and not for any incidental quality.*
>
> Aristotle, *The Nicomachean Ethics*

To come clean, to start over, to win
confidence—a man in spurs and chaps, or someone

on your side regardless. To be
known. That's how I explain to myself

what she slipped in
my hands, my desk drawer,

and my mouth was full of it. What
I can't explain my body

remembers and my body remembers
dreams of flight in those days, soaring wingless

above Buicks, treetops, the tesserae of lakes,
banking for my tenement, everything

needed to sustain the journey
contained in my body. The inarticulate joy of it.

How much easier to remember
than not to forget. The sight of Kay

and her sure step crossing
the newsroom floor, the street, it moves

me and everyone
is crazy about Kay, but the words

are everything between us.
I've forgotten so many words.

7 EAST 12th ST.

What I remember and what I don't
want to forget are not the same.

Kay and I live
a block apart and walk

12th Street home from work, car
radios and boomboxes

dividing the city.
It isn't a bad year

for music—Blondie's "Heart of Glass."
Pointer Sisters' "Fire."

The Village People.
The Police.

I think I have time to tell
Kay everything, time to ascend

together the steep rue
des Martyrs where she once

lived as did fierce St. Denis
who harvested his beheaded

head then trudged ten miles yapping
about Jesus. I can talk that way

about Kay, who makes hymnal worms
feel worthwhile.

One lunch hour we let the world end
leaning against our green granite

office exterior. The black coin of sun
has its day and for once I'm in sync

with everyone, their passing
shadows shrink like the recently dead,

diminutive
when the body stops. This pause

of darkness, my element and moment—
But the universe slips back into its groove

and we, eclipsed ourselves, return to the third floor
through the lobby, past the souring

patriarchs in dark oils. Even they
will be brought down. Change murders me

over and over again.

An annular solar eclipse
appeared on August 22, 1979

Maybe I'm imagining the whole thing.
What I'm sure of

Make the worst of what you've done
luminous marries me

to Kay. *Make the worst*
luminous bangs around inside

the sinus caves of my body. It is August
and we've come from the Bolshoi,

resonant with doom, Prokofiev's tune
throwing gauntlets at our feet.

The Montagues and Capulets

When I'm the age I am
writing this,

Romeo & Juliet no longer
makes me weep. Tragedy,

a confluence of events
that could have been

avoided, infuriates me. Bumbling Friar
Lawrence, a frustration beyond

expression—I'd scratch him
out of the cast and canon. What does

bring me to my knees
is inexpressible, a dancer's

slow solo in diffuse light, this beautiful
velvet seat right

beside me, empty, without
you, in the fourth ring.

Don't be afraid of who you are.

> "[Homosexuals] might be the most oppressed
> people in the society." — *Huey Newton, 1970*

Exiting the subway, the dance
is still inside

my head and your body and I love the ruby embrace
of the ribbon at your waist, how

the streets become your golden ballroom
and open their arms, a Champs-Élysées,

despite the unfashionable cars sidling
the curb while their rough drivers scavenge

for mouths of girls, who by dawn collapse in heaps
against the dirty glass of the Chinese

corner laundry as if wanting
to be taken in with the wash. *Don't be afraid.*

The dance is within us both. Here's
the upbeat, here the refrain,

The Montagues and Capulets

here my sandstone stoop, a garden
of colored crack vials. Goodnight. Goodnight.

He tao rakau he taea te karo—he tao korero e kore e taea.

A blow from a spear can be parried. A blow from words cannot.

Maori proverb

Redemption,
the word I keep forgetting.

Asti's singing waiter palming
sugared almonds like quarters

outside the red restaurant door we pass
leaving work every day.

The delight of friendship promises
such things, and the gravity of my colonized

body lifts, my grimy past
put to the furnace.

> colonize: to establish a colony in or on or
> of <e.g., the parasitic roundworms . . .
> have succeeded in *colonizing* a great
> variety of hosts – W. H. Dowdeswell>

If I define the terms, if I say
I haven't been

colonized or conquered, if I
separate my idea of myself

from the body, the bone
and tissue, and what's been

done with it
and what I've allowed

and what I could not
control, this body, the vestment

that has kept me
warm as it could, if I shutter

all the disgraces with the newsprint
copy of my 1970

Our Bodies, Ourselves
in the top shelf of my file cabinet, scraped

and dented and so unbeautiful, if I can
paw off the stain

of men laying claim
and women—I can't even count them

or their ratty Avenue B
sofas, their zebra-striped

hotel sheets, the complexity of desire
and the necessity of shelter—

and I jam in all the filth
ever whispered into our school girls'

ears as we made innocent
visits to grandmas or classrooms, girls stung

by indecencies on their own streets or
at home while cooking canned

mushroom soup and never able
to have mushroom soup

again, their colonial history
is my history and so extensive I can't stop puking

it up, I can't live with
its head low hanging

in that cabinet. But I can be
a new nation, indivisible, if only

I can remember Kay's
redemptive words.

> To grasp Earth's place in the universe,
> James Cook sailed for Tahiti
> where it was thought viewing conditions
> of the Transit of Venus were optimal.
> He arrived two months early.
> The following year, 1769, Cook set off
> for *terra australis incognita* only
> to discover there was no such
> Southern Continent balancing
> the northern hemisphere. Cook did
> find the Maori living in Aotearoa,
> which an earlier Dutch seaman
> called New Zealand. The encounter
> between British and Maori
> initiated a terrible void
> for the Maori. European colonizers
> would import firearms, alcohol,
> disease and prostitution, as well
> as missionaries, non-indigenous plants
> and animals, all of which would begin
> an unraveling of culture. The British arrival
> would decimate the Maori population
> by half.
>
> No angels lived here. When the Maori first
> settled on the two islands, how easy
> to capture and kill the flightless
> native birds, which clothed and fed
> the people. Many birds, some larger than our

wild turkeys, before being hunted
to extinction, sacrificed their skins
to cover the Maori women's breasts,
which the women deliberately exposed
in a display of venal disdain
(akin to our more frivolous mooning)
before disembarking Europeans.
How misinterpreted the exchange,
as if the men, driven by desire
for fruits of any kind, gave a damn.

Before Kay ventures south, we ride away
from a co-worker's funeral singing

this year's disco hit. Gloria
Gaynor bolsters the carpool

of us. Windows rolled down
though October has come in

snarling, it's easy
convincing one another

"I've got all my life to live."

Kay and I
sing that song,

"I Will Survive," though I don't
really care one way or another

and neither of us eat
the bologna roll-ups after mass.

There's a bad smell at the Red Apple
grocery on Fourth Avenue. Is it an accusation?

Great herons flap out the Third Street
Men's Shelter windows bloodying faces

of our rookie cops when they turn out
to be folding chairs. Why remember this

East Village mayhem where I am
home, the menacing

helicopters that hover like giant cockroaches,
the months the homeless women got

their throats cut and lived, the city tarring over
the last bit of history, Second Avenue's

Belgian setts, though we call them
cobblestones, the smog we eat all

summer at street fairs? Kay and I live
here. Decades after

I've moved away,
and I move when the pyramids of loss crush

me, every step and stone a cutting
reminder,

our shabby park will boast
a "state-of-the-art dog run,"

my $200/month studio will rent for
fourteen times this, apartments in Kay's building

at 170 Second Avenue, the one handsome
prewar in the neighborhood, fetch

million-dollar prices. For now, the sun
that never put its foot through

Binibon crowns Kay on these streets. In five years
everyone will be gone. Another day, Kay,

I'll talk to you about AIDS, which carts off
Harry Kondoleon, Tony Holland, John Duka

and Jeff, the blond Click model from Minnesota
who visits by fire

escape with his three Maltese
in tow, always referring to his shock over my

not owning an iron. Could anyone turn
to constellations for conversation

with dead friends? The massacre
of AIDS leaves us living

too busy swabbing crap and shoveling
another friend under. Loneliness gets no tip-toe

in. And the dead are too damn tired
to utter another word. They won't talk

to me. I believe when he is finished
only my dog

will be with me
the way books I've read are

with me, the way craters
are with the moon, congenital disease

with family. My nostalgia
for the East Village

will be a measure of impatience
with those who've come after

carrying luggage and lamps and no interest in us
or my father's electric flight suit.

> *Let no one live*
> *in oblivion*

By the close of the seventies so many are mugged
it's hard to believe

Year	Robberies	Population
1965	28,182	18,073,000
1979	**93,471**	17,650,000
2011	28,396	19,465,197

we hold on and love
our neighborhood of dubious Ukrainians, soup plates

Yiddish actors bend over at the Kiev, peddlers
at Cooper Square selling trash we put out only

an hour ago, quarrelling Puerto Rican social club members, men
and women pissing on the sidewalk, drug dealers in undershirts and fists

full of bills and joints on 9th Street, Italian pastry chefs with their moody
brood and biscotti. My East Village. I turn away and everyone shuffles

off the newsroom floor, the teletype stills. No one remains
who can help me fill in your contours. Our copy boy

with his carrot juice and martial arts
overdosed in a stairwell . . . Anita, HR's Sophia Loren,

a brain tumor . . . my boss Bernie Lett, Guadalcanal vet,
overflowed with cancer . . . heart disease choked Joe Mazo

with whom you worked elbow to elbow . . .
Mary in middle age with skirts slit to the armpit

sank under surgical complications . . . Good Howard
Kissel, who explained everything to nobodies

like me and theatre to everyone who was anyone, couldn't
survive despite the liver transplant.

Only funny Susie who says I never should have left
can help remember but all she does

remember is Kay's desk "on the perimeter of the newsroom,
where the interesting people sat—and my god

remember Phyllis Tweel!" who was photographed
by Mapplethorpe.

And where's the Dardanelles at 86 University Place, now
a rice-and-beans joint with no sorrowful

Armenian music? Am I alone
remembering Kay, chin on her fists, waiting

for copy and reading Merton, the disheveled other
three copyeditors awash in coffee, cigarettes and Jimmy Breslin?

—Can't any schmo tell you all this? Who's grilling me,
questioning what calls Kay to this crumbling

city, whether she has aspirations
as a painter, writer, trapeze artist?

I'm a dunce. I confess
I no longer remember why Kay would've come.

It is said throughout the seventies
New York has nothing

to offer but music. But so much
music—saxes, Patti Smith and hi-hats, amps and violins

are everywhere! Subways, back streets,
clubs, brick-stubbled lots. But it's the all-American

FORD TO CITY: DROP DEAD

Vows He'll Veto Any Bail-Out

Abe, Carey
Rip Stand

Stocks Skid,
Dow Down 12

anthems of jazz that stir
Kay, though she reminds everyone (she's heard it

a dozen times) of Anya
in *The Cherry Orchard.* See her in

churchy rapture, head bowed at Sweet Basil.
Fat Tuesday's. The Cookery. Bradley's. Kay

at the Village Vanguard. The Bitter End.

Everyone shakes it in our dark assemblies, CBGBs,
the Academy of Music, Studio 54, the Mudd Club,

the Pyramid, Irving Plaza. We hustle and thrash
in black and black until the seventies go

white as a hospital bed, white
as polar ice,

the decade shuddering,
1979, its garage

door rolling
down, a total whiteout, exeunt,

escorting Kay under
its blank arm.

The year is one
of extremes and extremities.

For thirty minutes snow falls
in the Sahara, science fiction's

meltdown becomes science fact
at Three Mile Island,

and we find Etan Patz
on every city bus.

Whatever weird star arranged our meeting
is not what will pull us apart.

But at both ends
I say Hosannas.

*Make the worst
of what you've done luminous,* Kay says, part

prayer, part mantra, far better
than five Hail Marys. I don't know this

is our last time, last stroll, last casual
conversation, which always effervesces

yet with arms raised to the Guardian Life
building, Hosanna!

Hosanna to our streetlamp procession, Hosanna
to windows winking at us walking home.

To our magnetic poles, Hosanna. Hosanna to drawing us
close in my helpless age.

To this brief transit, finding a place
in the universe, Hosanna.

Hosanna, Hosanna, Hosanna
to being afraid of so much love

as saucers of snow spin diagonally
through the canyon of Second Avenue. Hosanna!

FLIGHT TE901

Things get off to a bad start.
The aircraft's departure

is delayed twenty minutes when
a woman on board freaks

out, wants off. She's
unsettling to some, to some

gently amusing. What kingdom's soft muzzle
whispers prophecy in her ear?

The crew allows her to
disembark. The terminal

staff calms her, reassures her, and
she reboards. She reboards

because life is exploration—
or decay.

CRUISING ALTITUDE

First farewell to the farmland
below, green as billiard cloth.

Then the knobby alpine spine
down New Zealand's South

Island falling astern while the ship
continues to climb. Soon

the gray comfortless
Southern Ocean, the widebody going over

its faceless expanse.
For a diversion, the pop! of Champagne

and the breakfast service begins, accompanied by
three polar documentaries, including 1964's

140 Days Under the World. Over
the tremendous sea, the DC-10's shadow

a flea upon it. Sighting
the grassland of Disappointment

Island relieves the tourist's lingering
despair—the possibility

of land! of landing! And gone. Visit
the flight deck. More Champagne

uncorked and the cabin's amok
with goodwill, sunglasses, binoculars.

This is the life.

The fearful passage
of their death-mark'd love

Cameras whir and snap

to action at this masked
ball, this sky-flying cocktail

party. Inward types cozy up to
diaries . . . two hundred shutterbugs . . .

some enter sanctuary with Eliot Porter's
coffee table *Antarctica* in their laps—then

a reverent hush as the aircraft approaches
the ice continent.

Unbuckle, passengers! Lumber
up and down aisles like zombies. Exchange

seats. Silly woman lugging your fur, now
is the time to dress for snow.

Politely they jockey
for a starboard view. Shutters

click. Movie cameras pan,
ratcheting steadily. It's a peep-show

at the portholes while the cockpit
checks for waypoints. Clear

skies at Balleny Islands, Cape Adare, then
Cape Hallett, McMurdo Sound,

Cape Royds, Cape Bernacchi.
Antarctica!

Bigger than the US by half.
Antarctica, where from its heart

any direction traveled
is north.

Tourists, the snaps you take
will testify

to more than you
know. Thousands of frames show

fair visibility at altitude, perfect
for the polar trickery

that paints a snowy mountain with ice
from above as one

foggy curtain. Flat light
whiteout. This evidence

will deconstruct disaster. So too
the movie camera that sweeps

the cabin to linger
on a young woman like Kay but not

Kay. I've played and replayed
the film clip so many times

but never find her
in the color-rinsed footage the desert

cold preserved. Is she aft of the lens, viewing
Ross Island's absinthe-tinted ice,

the logical plaid of the calving
frozen sheets, this fragile hairline

where ice edge meets open water?
Perhaps she's right before my eyes

in one of these faded seats. Kay's no
taller than I. Perhaps

the seat back obscures her, she's
not strolling the aisles but buckled in,

as all experienced aviators, my father
or Kay's mother, always urge. Belted in

this misadventure, you're unlikely to be ripped
from the fuselage with those who'll be found

littering the ice like beachgoers,
short-sleeved and shoeless, almost dozing.

Ladies and gentlemen, the
captain has turned off the Fasten
Seat Belt sign and you're free to
move around the cabin.
However, we recommend
keeping your seat belt fastened
while seated . . .

Ladies and gentlemen, where you think you are
is 27 miles west of where

you actually are.
This wouldn't matter if

TE901 were winging McMurdo Sound's
open water.

Instead you're flying over
land booby-trapped

by Mt. Terror and Mt. Erebus
on an altered flight plan.

If only you weren't coming in
on your knees

but Air New Zealand's Antarctic flights do
swoop low and

TE901 requests
the go ahead

from McMurdo Air Traffic to descend
below 2000 feet.

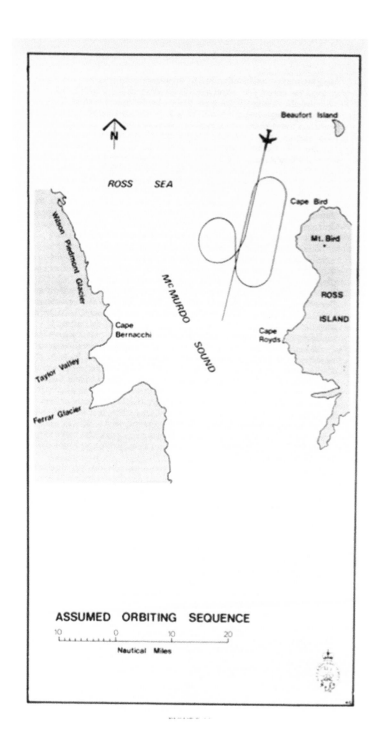

Beaufort Island

N

ROSS   SEA

Wilson Piedmont Glacier

Cape Bird

Mt. Bird

McMURDO

ROSS

ISLAND

Cape
Bernacchi

Cape
Royds

SOUND

Taylor Valley

Ferrar Glacier

ASSUMED ORBITING SEQUENCE

10   0   10   20

Nautical Miles

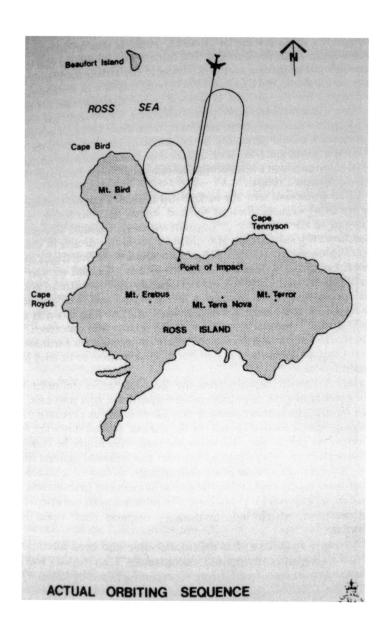

ACTUAL ORBITING SEQUENCE

and so approved,
the orbiting sequence begins,

first turning to the right
then an elegant loop to the left,

taking you down
thousands and thousands more

feet from an altitude of 10,000
to 1,500 feet.

Mt. Erebus   elevation: 12,447 feet

The sightseeing hardly begun yet the journey
is nearly done. The DC-10

so quiet in the sky has only minutes
before meeting Erebus. Because

what you see is not the black scarp of Cape
Royds but Cape Tennyson,

not Cape Bernacchi but
Cape Bird, the water below

not the flat sea ice of McMurdo Sound
but Lewis Bay, gateway to Erebus. The way

is not clear. Though Ross Island's high terrain
stands far and safely east

of the briefing route,
Air New Zealand changed

the computer coordinates
at 1:40 this morning, before the flight,

and no one on board
has been told.

This is why craft and crew fly two
separate routes.

The course is set.
Prepare for departure.

Marion cannot feel easy
hearing uncertainty in Mulgrew's voice

as to their position while the aircraft swings so
sweet chariot low

in visually uncertain
terrain. Did she

give Kay a look
or did she have every confidence in her

fellow pilots? In Air
New Zealand's own

magazine, sightsees regularly drop low
as robin red breasts when a-nesting.

Guide Peter Mulgrew
(12:45)
This is Peter Mulgrew speaking
again folks. I still can't see very much
at the moment. Keep you
informed soon as I see something
that gives me a clue
as to where we are.
We're going down
in altitude now and it won't be long
before we get quite a good . . . .

Flight Engineer to Mulgrew
(12:46)
Where's Erebus in relation to us at the moment?

Mulgrew
Left, about four or five miles, eleven o'clock.

Flight Engineer
I'm just thinking of any high ground in the area, that's all.

Mulgrew
I think it'll be left.

Flight Engineer
Yes, I reckon about here.

Mulgrew
Yes . . . no, no, I don't really know.

Captain
(12:47)
Actually, those conditions don't look very good at all.

Mulgrew
No they don't.

Flight Engineer
I don't like this.

Captain
We'll have to climb out of this.

First Officer
You're clear to turn right. There's no high ground if you do a one eighty.

Captain
No . . . negative.

The terrain alarm
Whoop, whoop. Pull up. Whoop whoop.

Flight Engineer
Five hundred feet.

Terrain alarm
Pull up.

Flight Engineer
Four hundred feet.

Terrain alarm
Whoop, whoop. Pull up. Whoop whoop. Pull up.

Captain
Go-around power please.

Terrain alarm
(12:49)
Whoop, whoop. Pull—

Transcript excerpts from the Cockpit Voice Recorder

(Sundstrand Model B serial #256 Part # 980-6005-061)

McMurdo Air Traffic expects the DC-10
to fly over momentarily. The great birds usually
come in fast and low, sightseers
reaping their money's worth.

But McMurdo gets no
flyby. Snow hard as sugar
on the ground, skies heavy with
cloud cover, visibility 40 miles.

Kiwi New Zealand
niner zero one
doesn't arrive. The controller suspects,
with McMurdo overcast, TE901 rerouted

for clearer skies. But when time passes
without any transmission,
Air Traffic knows something
isn't right. The rule of the skies

requires radioing a position report
every fifteen minutes, thirty at most.
It's been an hour. McMurdo can't raise
New Zealand niner zero one.

They have been released
from hundreds of hands

yet cameras keep filming after
impact. In that tick of time, less

than it takes the heart to beat,
most passengers

are thrown from the plane—
few had been belted

in. The fuselage continues galloping
up the mountain, disintegrating

for more than 300 meters, thrusting
even more bodies out as it gouges a path,

until the skeletal alloy comes
to rest. Then, the incineration.

But nobody anywhere has any idea
this has happened to you. Not yet.

No one in the world hears

    metal claw ice
or the retort when the craft explodes.

No one in the world sees

    bodies catapulted into crevasse
after crevasse

    cleaved by the wreck as it hurtled
along ice, the dying animal furiously burrowing

    passengers into frozen tombs. A hand in shifting snow
seems to imitate the royal wave, not wanting

    to make a fuss.

No one in the world has the acrid taste of the inferno

    in the soft pink tissue
of the mouth.

Who could have stood such witnessing

    at the bootsole of the world?
And yet we want to

    go to the hyperboreal
landscape and scrape some

    badge of visitation there,
an X marks the spot. For what?

    Claim it for the queen, claim it
for the tsar. For God or money

            or tell me why
people are driven to cry out, This

            is where I am!

The simpleton's way
to grasp the number of lives lost

calls for envisioning
one corpse you love

at every yard line
for the length of

three football fields. How well
every sports metaphor I've ever heard

captures the high stakes
of deception and brutality.

If the number of the dead
doesn't suck on your breath, consider

what it meant in New Zealand,
try to find a Kiwi of a certain age

who didn't know someone on that plane
personally or by association

or who can't recall their own
whereabouts when the news jimmied in.

The most haunting photo in the history of flight
TE901 is shot the instant

death cuts in line. The photo is
the affidavit of 257 souls.

In the "final photograph of actual impact,"
writes an investigator, the fluid depicted
on the aircraft's windows is thought
to be jet fuel, which ignited the inferno.

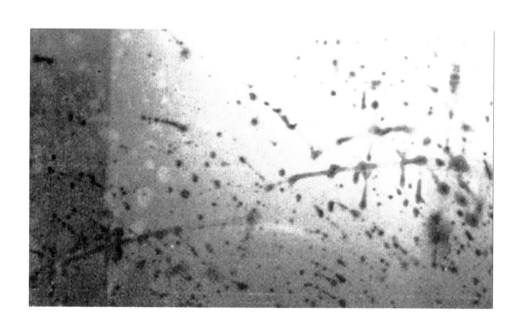

By the time the photographer
released the shutter, she was dead.
Investigators viewed additional
still shots and moving
footage. In the dark
the projector

screened images of interior cabin shots,

clumsy

amateur swings around

to the window, the amazed tourist's

frames

of ice below. And then.

An interruption of flames.

The silence.

Blurry objects tumbling. The silence

of Super 8.

Then blackness.

Maybe I can't find you in any film
because you aren't on the flight after all.

Maybe I've come to understand what it means to hope
against hope.

It is Wednesday
in Antarctica, near midnight,

when the American helicopter
from McMurdo Base spots

the comet-like streak
careening up the lower slope

of Mt. Erebus. Weather conditions
make landing out of the question

and for what purpose? It's clear
to the Major

there are no survivors
down here.

In New York it is
only Tuesday.

On Tuesday
you two were on the bed

in your mother's hotel room
eating macadamias.

My news director pulls it off
the wire. Or does your brother

call the office? Someone has the courage to announce
your plane has been lost

over Antarctica. No one says crashed
and burned. No one says no survivors. Am I dense

or just twenty-five to think if you're lost
you're in suspension above the Pole

in centrifugal flight, you're unharmed,
you're the Girl

with the Pearl Earring
looking inscrutably out at us,

Kay at the porthole, endlessly circling the Pole.
No comfort, no solace. It's even worse

than flat out dead or that hoary thing,
deceased. Oh, I've eaten bad

fish! newsroom dims, floor buckles, but not
one head bows down, no candle sniffles

in any corner, no skirts rip
at the seam and I don't know where

                                                    I belong.

My dog, my dog—the animals have seen this
kind of thing before. Good shepherd, please explain.

In the first *New York Times* report
you are misidentified

> BARNICK, Miss D.
> BARNICK, Miss M.

The hurt of happiness at finding you alive
in the lost flight is tempered by

questions. Whose awful passport belongs to
D. Barnick? And where does that leave you? Shivering blue

on the glacial tongue? I hate to think of you
who were envied

by our fashion reporters for your natural
good looks and pompadour

on the slope, your
French hairpin skidding across frozen ground.

> *The earth's coldest temperature,*
> *-128° F, is recorded at*
> *Antarctica's Vostok Station*

Don't be lonely.

> In 1908
Ernest Shackleton's team hiked

to the rim of Erebus
though the boss hung back in his survival

hut. Fifty years later, a graceless convoy of tractors
hauled Hillary to that hut

where he was warmly received by
Shackleton's ghost.

"I distinctly saw Shackleton walking
towards me and welcoming me."

Who can doubt Sir Edmund Hillary
when he says he's seen a ghost?

You're not alone. Robert Scott's on the continent
too, potted in silent centuries of

ice.

Kathleen Scott, wife of the man who died trying
to be first to cross the South Pole,
cheered on the Royal Navy officer
with a penciled note slipped into
his coat pocket:
"If there's anything worth doing
at the cost of your life—

do it . . . How awful if you don't."

Robert Falcon Scott did
reach the Pole, in January 1912,
a month after Amundsen
      and it was at the cost
of his life and the lives
      of his four men. Scott's team, suffering
starvation, frostbite and scurvy,
      wouldn't survive
the return home. That November
      a search party, finding Scott
beside his team, buried the explorer
      beneath his tent on the Ross Ice
Shelf and memorialized him
      with a cairn of ice and snow.

Kathleen wanted her own tombstone
      to declare the world's happiest woman
lay below.

Does my dog tell me
in accepting the risks and traveling anyway,

even downhearted Scott
triumphed at the Pole? I believe that

to be true. But what do I know
about truth?

I've been lying
my entire life. It's all a parade—

brass horns, boot shine, confetti
and my heart outside in.

Don't be afraid of who
you are.

This is the end
of my heartbroken life

I thought when I met Kay,
and it was, for a moment,

and it was a break
in the weather. Pick up

the phone, pick up. Don't take that
step into oblivion. I know something's wrong

with me. Friends, Romans, countrymen

Bear with me;
My heart is in the coffin there with Caesar,
And I must pause till it come back to me.

and family insist it's time
I "get over it." Kay, come

home, unpack your luggage. Show me
travel photographs. Who vanishes for good

behind the magician's black cape? Already
I can't remember the music

of your voice.

That's it. No funeral or obit.
Am I the only one

who can't understand
what's happened to you? Even

my dog isn't compelled to search
and rescue you. Your building stands unmoving.

I see it from my corner. In your apartment, your shoes
patient as little sphinxes. Cookbooks

and magazines doze,
tongues hanging out, the bath towel

that knew you so intimately,
exhausted on the rack.

Of course I'm going to run
into you again and jumping-jack

outside the Pharmacy's plate glass window
as you brunch, fork to lips, on Avenue A.

Of course I'll see you and your sfogliatelle at De Roberti's
again, and again in line at the Public Theatre, my heart

bam bamming like a parent reconnecting
with lost children in the park. But why

haven't you shown yet? I understand
we make a mouth in the earth

and lay the bodies in
to convince ourselves

the dead won't come back to us.
But isn't our graveside sorrow

half a cup of hope
for their return?

The blood
banks, Cinema Village, the Strand, Paterson Silks,

Lüchow's, Bowlmor, parking garages, the Police
Athletic League, Stromboli's, Asti's, Teddy's coffee shop—

as I wander past our old haunts,
these buildings boldly weep

for you, waiters wave gray dishrags, *"Yassou,*
where your friend?" "Ciao! Where . . .?" and a shrug.

I pretend not to hear but how long
can that go on?

The most logical response—to tell everyone you
moved. It will tie all ends up with twine.

If I tell people (you died), what
then? Will they

try to make me feel better, want details, give me
my coffee and bran muffin on the house?

The thing is, I haven't yet said it
out loud. Next time when the Greeks ask

where the hell are you? what comes
out is, "I don't know," and it's the truth and then I surrender

to the wrecking ball of it all. Your handwriting,
your voice, the color of your eyes. I am failing this

test because what does death do
but make of someone three-dimensional two?

EVENT OF AN EMERGENCY

The American hostages in Teheran hang
from a brace over the bar.

At a holiday party
someone pounds Prokofiev from the baby

grand, middle E sluggish
as the clinically depressed

but more noticeable. I'm waiting for somebody
to bring good news

from Antarctica but there's nothing of the frozen
world. It is done. "Silent Night"

mewls from the piano when I creep
toward that cast iron harp

to cut its strings.

DAMAGE CONTROL I

(American search aircraft from McMurdo, taking advantage of the continent's 24-hour daylight, trace the sightseer's flight path. Not a sign of a wreck. No ice hole where she might've gone under. No bright flotation device. No survivors waving hankies. The news is relayed to Air New Zealand corporate headquarters.)

Flight 901, where the bloody hell are you? A Chivas would be nice right now. Of course, we didn't say a word to the fact the Yanks might be looking in the wrong place. They never liked us flying over the ice to begin with. In case just a thing like this . . . extreme remote . . . inhospitable environment . . . and all that. But an outstanding opportunity for the airline business, you must agree.

Could be engine failure. Like last May in Chicago. American Airlines Flight 191. Engine #1 plumb fell off, right out of the skies during takeoff. McDonnell-Douglas boys will be screwed if that's the case. At least it won't be our fault. Be curtains for the DC-10.

I'll wager 901 lost their way in thick cloud cover. Whatever, the company's not going down for this. No way in bloody hell.

On 2 December 1979 Morrie Davis,
Air New Zealand's CEO, admits

to a (New Zealand) *Sunday Times*
journalist, "the effect of the accident

on our reputation
which has been unblemished

for 40-odd years," weighs on him
like his immense eyeglasses. Davis, the public face

of the airline, can't hide his "tough
gamecock" personality from the reporter.

"We have to remain viable
as an enterprise

that demonstrably has an integrity
as good as any

and better than most."
On his desk the international headlines

say otherwise: DC10 CRASH
WITH 257 *LA Herald Examiner;*

257 FEARED DEAD IN ANTARCTIC
CRASH *Honolulu Star Bulletin.*

Earlier in the week Mr. Davis insists
it "insignificant" the lost pilots

had no Antarctic experience.
His Australian competitor Qantas,

which flew more than two dozen
sightsees over the continent,

allows only crew with polar
training to command such expeditions.

When the Navy at McMurdo discover
this fact, they're aghast—the US Navy,

aghast? Hearing of the crash and death
of his companion Mulgrew,

Hillary responds, "Those things happen,
I suppose" then marries

Mulgrew's widow. My defensive
driving instructor, whose career rests on

what is and what is not
avoidable,

would never have called this
an accident.

ac´ci`dent late 14th c. from Old
French via Latin (*ad*
"to" + *cadere* "fall");
literally, a befalling

an unforeseen,
unplanned event;
chance; undesigned
occurrence usually
afflictive in nature;
injurious event without
an apparent cause

euphemistic reference
to an involuntary act or
instance of urination
or defecation

(*Gram.*) A property
attached to a word,
but not essential to
it, as gender, number,
case.

(*Her.*) A point or mark
which may be retained
or omitted in a coat of
arms

(*Log.*) A property
or quality of a thing
which is not essential
to it, as whiteness in
paper; an attribute.

DAMAGE CONTROL II

How do you promise a sightsee if you don't allow your pilots to descend low? Just don't admit this at Inquiry. Pilot's discretion we always say.

Make damn sure the public understands it didn't matter one whit that we tweaked the navigation settings before the flight. The aircraft flew directly at the volcano? The pilots were never told of the nav track change? (Shrug)

Write that accident report in secret. Present it to the public just before the Royal Inquiry gets its story out. Suggest to the press a mysterious flight-deck illness. Transcribe the voice recorder to indicate confusion in the cockpit. You know what I'm saying. Do I have to say it in plain English? Blame the pilots. Blame the fucking pilots.

Orchestrate a burglary the bloody second the captain's family leaves that house of mourning. Send someone into that house, I don't know who, crikey! How about a bloody grief counselor? Gather the papers. Shred shred shred. Bloody Antarctica! Should some mongrel vandalize the bedside photo of the captain and his wife I'll know nothing of it! There shall be no discrepancy between the briefing flight path and the computerized path. Ditch the diary pages from the pilot's binder.

Have someone leave the captain's uniform on the widow's doorstep. A brown paper bag will do. We need to show some feelings. After all, at Air New Zealand we're a kind of family, no?

OXYGEN MASK WILL DROP

What a hoarse wind
   staggers this
      silence Men are falling
         out of the colorless
            from hanging pianos
               Is that how we came

to be in this place Hideously
   they move toward us
      What do they want
         Are they drunk Are they
            Frankensteins Conquistadores Migrating

Angels Here they come Why
   carry weapons Don't they realize O
      rope pickaxes and little flags
         snapping in the wind Look
            how earnest they are Why
               hammering It's too late for

gallows Don't let them
      bury us here Mother It's cold Are you
         cold What are they building Men love
            making noise So much noise
               It's a platform A dance
                  floor Let's dance It will keep us

warm Now what Why
   are they collecting
      our weird tribe They're having a time of it Aren't they
         Smoking looting booze ransacking pockets and
            Hey handsome Why won't they I've heard
               murderers too don't look you in the eyes

Kay we won't stay
long Don't we always
return home
eventually

Let's go dancing Mother Surely
they'll have music I'd love to listen
to some jazz right now I can't
budge Can you Here comes another
big guy Doesn't he look like he's just
seen a ghost This cold This cold

makes me drowsy How's that
flight plan coming Mother
Mother are you still
there I can't turn my If you are
please say something
Answer

Some folks seem to be hearing pipe
organs and boy choirs I hear a drone
steady and pitch
perfect Gracious It's my
Cessna the 172 and there's
the Ercoupe that won me
first prize Now where
did I stow those
macadamias I keep
a jar on board
every plane

First what confusion then
insurmountable
sadness Not as definitive
as grief A feeling I'll never get out
but the song O no not I

I can see
    Are my eyes open or closed I am
        the light that takes all morning
            to move across the study
                wall I can be the sun
                    warmed fruit in your palm

    Kay here is Mother Here
    we go now Upsa daisy Gentlemen don't forget
    my beautiful daughter She's my
    oldest I had her somewhere She's the one
    with the heart the magnificent
    heart and her hair Kay usually wears it
    up Gibson girl style You're too young
    to know what I'm talking about Kay
    raise a hand so the young
    men can find you She was right
    beside me a second ago I'm sorry
    Say again Negative It's hard
    to hear in the wind Negative
    Her hair isn't burnt
    umber It's gold silver and butter
    scotch Perhaps it's all undone
    and loose to her waist

Someone's come I'm in
    his arms And now it's time
        It's time to stop
            thinking in words
                Mother
                  goodbye
                      It's time to It's time

    Death is only this night
    flying the instrument panel
    aglow in your eyes beside me
    Keep moving Keep flying Amelia
    wrote If I should bop off

it'll be doing the thing that I've
always most wanted to do
We chose to be adventurers
to journey from here to Flaps up
Full throttle Wheels in the well
On to brighter horizons!

New Zealand police and mountain
rescue team are flown to Antarctica.

In my ignorance my image of the disaster
in the locket of my memory

remains pristine: Kay vanishing
in boundless, eternal Antarctic white.

I couldn't have been more wrong. There is no
heavenly circumnavigation

but a DC-10 that flew as programmed,
a missile into the mountain.

Let the soot people
filter through me,

the fine ash that was
a silk scarf, a full lip, an index finger, come.

And come, all the mysteriously misplaced
evidence. The dozens of photographs

passengers shot from the south
that prove whiteout conditions. Come

briefing notes and marketing
materials and four minutes of erased

air traffic tape. Come, you
burglar who stole papers but no

jewelry from the dead
pilot's home. Come you crooks

who've died disgraced
by your own darkness. Come

everyone into this
endlessness. Let me be

a better friend than I was when
those know-nothings

told me I had mourned
enough. Grieving has only

begun in America.

In the late 1980s I stood in the St. Marks Bookshop
reading. I didn't want to
know about a toxic gas leak
from Union Carbide's pesticide plant
outside Bhopal, India, in 1984
but I couldn't stop reading.

The hardboiled egg eyes.
Cats. Dogs. Cows. Buffaloes.
Fallen over in the streets
like taxidermy or porcelain
figurines tipped off their feet,
an apocalypse of birds
shaken from the blue.

In the immediate aftermath, thousands
died, tens of thousands more
would follow, hundreds of thousands
permanently injured.

International courts accuse
the chemical king of inadequate compensation,
of responsibility for the disaster,
shoddy safety standards.

I wanted you in that
bookstore, Kay, balance beam Kay,
tidying up the world and calming
the bewildered beasts whose horns
point toward oblivion.

Union Carbide's website blames
a saboteur
but refuses to name him "because
it would serve no useful purpose."

Union Carbide is a wholly owned subsidiary
of Dow Chemical, the company that brought us
napalm and Agent Orange.

Kay, was that you in the bookshop reading
over my shoulder? Did you hover without
flapping your wings? Was that you murmuring?
Make the worst luminous and write?

Until 2012, when I began to write about the Erebus crash, all I knew of the catastrophe was from the uncertain *New York Times* article and news at work. The scene, in my mind, remained pristine, like space debris.

From my subsequent research, most candid are the accounts of those who were part of the recovery effort. Nothing could have prepared me for the devastation I encountered there.

Nothing could have prepared us for the devastation we encountered.

Skua gulls were eating the bodies. This hampered victim identification. We tried to shoo them. We lobbed emergency flares. Nothing scared them off. Nothing. Even after corpses were bagged, the gulls tore through the body bags to pull at the flesh.[1]

The flight had been equipped with a well-stocked bar and some of the liquor on board survived the crash. After all the labor was done, we made use of it.

---

1 Antarctic veteran Bernie Gunn, who visited the continent as a PhD student as part of Edmund Hillary's team in the 1950s, has this to say about the skua gulls: "Skuas are unlovely creatures[;] one hopes God feels affection for them because few people do. They are ruthless scavengers, nest close to penguin rookeries so they can steal eggs or young chicks, hover round seals with pups and may pick their eyes out. I never even shot one which shows either remarkable forbearance or dereliction of duty on my part. I cannot in my most generous moments believe that a world free of skuas would be all that worse off. My conscience is salved by the number of times I have biffed an ice-axe at one, not I regret, with much effect as several centuries of explorers biffing ice-axes at them has taught them to duck."

The slope was about 14°, too steep for the helos to land, so we built a landing platform into the mountain. When the helos came in, the winds sent fragments of torn metal objects flying in all directions.

We were soon to learn the dangers and suddenness of the changeable weather conditions. Without any real warning a severe storm blew up with gale force winds and snow. The temperature dropped with the wind chill factor to the vicinity of minus 40 degrees. After several hours the storm abated. On inspecting the crash site again it had changed considerably. Bodies and wreckage, which were previously visible, were now covered with snow, and others not visible initially were now exposed.

After handling so many charred bodies, our gloves had become completely saturated in black human grease.

Water being a rare resource, we washed our hands in a community basin. The water turned black as molasses. I couldn't eat the first meal anyway. Meat stew.

To keep a distance we had to joke about the remains—the "roasted meat," "wax works," "ice pops." The hardest part wasn't the disfigured or dismembered bodies. It was the intact ones. They made you think, "That could have been me. That could have been my wife, my daughter."

Among the victims' belongings was a dictionary. It was frozen open to a page where the first word I saw was "**corpse**."

The crash had cleaved open innumerable crevasses, bottomless to the eye. We tried abseiling but who thought to bring a flashlight in 24-hour daylight? I don't like to imagine what landed down there.

The sun that allowed the US military to search through the night until the DC-10 was found is the sun that offered no warmth to the recovery team. Yet any flesh unprotected by gear or cream burnt in no time.

One of my first tasks was to build a snow-dome toilet to help protect naked bums from the intense wind-chill swirling around the nether regions.

Immediately I was drawn to its wonders—the extreme cold (for me), the purity of the landscape, the clarity of the air, the tenacity of the wildlife, the ever-present dangers of the environment.

Our party travelled to the crash site and was met by the horrendous sight before us. Each body had been flagged (green) along with the perimeter of the site (black) and the crevasse edges (red), in case a storm were to cover the bodies with snow.

Throughout my time there, I had this underlying sadness of the lost potential and the utter waste of it all.

Antarctica 1979

_____

_____

_____

_____

_____

_____

_____

_____

_____

_____

_____

_____

_____

_____

I found myself reading people's diaries. Some of the entries will remain with me for the rest of my life.

One was headed up, "Antarctica 1979" but the page was blank.

Another, half written, described the trip so far and how beautiful the Antarctic was. The last words in the diary were, "Gee, it's great to be alive."

A perfect imprint of the DC-10's underbelly and wings lay in the snow at the bottom of the crash site. This indicated the aircraft was pulling up at the time of impact and disintegrated as it travelled up the mountain slope throwing those on board out as it went.

The crash site and the airspace above it have been officially designated a tomb. Period of designation: Indefinite. All pilots operating in the region are informed of over-flight restrictions, which include the airspace to an altitude of 1000 m (3280 ft). The region is inspected by national Antarctic programs as needed, but no less than every five years.

A six-foot Oregon-timber cross was installed near Erebus by late 1979 but nature wore it away in less than ten years.

Nigel Roberts had been two months at Scott Base when the directive arrived. He was to take only one camera and shoot only black-and-white.

As an information officer for New Zealand's Department of Scientific and Industrial Research, Roberts knew something was amiss when he heard the noise. Normally, it's immensely quiet in the Antarctic—no traffic, no car horns, no school kids playing ball, no birdsong, no wind blustering trees. Suddenly the air was filled with ignitions turning over in Land Rovers and jeeps, helicopters shuddering to life, and giant C-130 Hercules cargo planes growling on the runway. Flight TE901 had been found.

A helicopter brought Roberts over the crash site, and he went to work.

The reasoning behind the orders to carry one camera and not use color film was to lessen the chances the material might fall "into the wrong hands" (b/w film could be developed at the station; color required being sent to a commercial lab). Despite his limited resources, Roberts took some of the most iconic photographs of the Erebus crash, including the image of the tail with its distinctive koru logo, lying amputated in the snow.

I can't speak for any other police officers. Let's just say the support was not adequate. Things fell apart after fifteen years. Now it's thirty years since Antarctica and I haven't seen snow once.

Inspector Jim Morgan, who led the Auckland mortuary team, observed: "It was very difficult for our young police officers who may have handled the occasional sudden death to be confronted with 257 sudden deaths all at once. The young single people suffered some quite bad psychological trauma." Read about it:

Taylor, A.J.W. & Frazier, A.G. *Psychological sequelae of Operation Overdue following the DC10 aircrash in Antarctica* (1981). Wellington: Victoria University Publications in Psychology #27

More than a quarter century would pass before the country could collect itself to the point of issuing distinguished service medals to the scores of men and women who offered extraordinary assistance in response to the Erebus crash. A number of Americans also received the medal.

2013

BRACE FOR IMPACT

The crash of Flight TE901
is the most devastating
peacetime disaster
the country has ever experienced.

Worse than
the landslide of 1780,
1863 blizzard,
the Great Storm of 1868,
countless shipwrecks,
collapsed buildings,
volcanic eruptions,
mine accidents,
lahar-flooded railways,
the Seacliff Lunatic Asylum fire in 1942,
1947 Ballantynes Department Store fire,
Mt. Ruapehu air crash in 1948 and a year later
one near Waikanae,
the Wellington-Lyttelton yacht race tragedy,
the 1955 ghost ship *Joyita*
sighted in the South Pacific
five weeks late and off course for Tokelau,
Northland bus crash and
Kaimai airline disaster in 1963,
Whanganui (1988), Milford Sound (1989)
and Franz Josef Glacier (1993) air crashes,
Cave Creek viewing-platform collapse in 1995,
Lindis Pass airplane crash in 2000,
Tongariro canyon drowning in 2008,
2010 skydiving crash at Fox Glacier
and Pike River coalmine tragedy,
2011 Christchurch earthquake,
and in 2012 the Carterton ballooning fire
and Foveaux Strait capsizing.

Disaster hits New Zealand
hard, a country smaller than
Vietnam, a country the size
of Colorado. But I'm tired
of comparisons.
Disaster is disaster.

El Nuevo Herald
27 de diciembre de 2000
La Habana se cae a pedazos por las lluvias

1963 L'ouragan «Flora» a tué plus de 8000 Haïtiens. Ce cyclone était considéré comme la 6e plus fort du XXe siècle sur le continent américain. Peu après le passage de «Flora», le pays a connu sa pire épidémie de paludisme.

1556 陝西地震死亡近 100 萬人死亡人數最多的地震紀錄

For superstitious
souls who fear
I've jinxed
New Zealand and myself
by mentioning the worst of the worst,
thinking fate will try
to outdo us,
this may be the time to
light the votive
chant with others
lay the knife by the pillow
clutch the crystal
knot the red thread at the wrist
worry the beads and rosaries
get down on your knees and
flagellate.

Because it's true. Things can get worse.

Be good to one another.

Grids marked the spot

where in daylight, at 12:50

in the afternoon, at the position

77° 25′ 30″ S and 167° 27′ 30″ E,

and an elevation of 1467 feet

above mean sea level,

a DC-10 in a controlled flight

drove into a mountain

and exploded into smithereens.

This set off a "persistent,

intense and deep seated [sic] fire."

The first of many reports
encountered three decades after Kay's absence

undoes my hope
she's living

with a single word.
Chief Inspector of Air Accidents

Ron Chippindale writes, "The accident was
unsurvivable." It's a word I've never seen

before. Forensic evidence leads
mortuary pathologists to concur.

The event was "not survivable
in any way." Learning death

wouldn't bargain, learning that
extinction offered no time for fright, does not

there-there me. And time
does not blunt the blow.

Who can conceive of
being buried by the initial crash, discovered

by recovery workers, reburied in the ice for safekeeping,
dug out and buried again? Handled, ogled,

photographed, pecked at,
re-buried, sampled, tagged, numbered and

transported multiple times
by helicopter, airplane, truck and dolly before

the head jarring
ceases for good?

Some are horrified to see
what I see, one of you a few yards from

the tail and #2 engine cowling
but just outside

the formal composition
Nigel Roberts made famous, arms

thrown back as if to dive into . . .
one leg strangely bent high

where the thigh should be. This cadaver
doesn't shock me. What did

people expect? A sanitation crew?
I love the body

as the vehicle
to get love through to you.

*Personal identification of unidentified bodies is crucial
for ethical, juridical and civil reasons
and is performed through comparison
between biological data obtained from the cadaver
and antemortem material from one or more missing persons
to whom the body may have belonged in life.*

Abstract from *La Radiologia Medica*

Before departing Antarctica
the knees, elbows and foreheads of the dead and more

than one hundred fragmented remains
are blessed by a US Navy chaplain

posted at Williams Field
during Operation Overdue.

Williams Field

a polar layer-cake
of an airstrip: at the
time, two runways
composed of 25 feet
of compacted snow
on top of 260 feet of
ice floating atop 1,800
feet of water serving
Scott Base (New
Zealand operated) and
McMurdo Station (US
operated)

Operation Overdue

code name for the
New Zealand police
and Mountain
Face Rescue Team
responsible for the
recovery effort of
flight TE901

Were they not already blessed
by the sweetness of the natural world

enraged and inhospitable
as it may seem

from time to time? If the fanged frozen Pole
is not the earth in balance, then what

else but a last cry
against our scratched and gutted

hell pits, our greasy spills that choke
what breeds in the seas?

Don't let me hear you
say these were sightseers who didn't care to

get their feet wet, who couldn't take the cold
in their teeth, who wanted spectacle and to be home

in time for their favorite
evening TV. These travelers were enamored

with the continent barely seen, the globe's skullcap,
a mere frill on maps. They had come to honor

the planet's crowning.

No one imagined
so many bodies

would be brought home yet
dozens remain in Antarctica.

When winds shift and snows melt,
who and what was irretrievably buried

by the DC-10 drilling into the ice
rise to the surface. These travelers,

with fellow explorer Scott and his
lost men, will in time be drawn home, to the sea.

All of us have in our veins
the exact same percentage of salt in our blood
that exists in the ocean, and therefore,
we have salt in our blood, in our sweat,
in our tears. We are tied to the ocean.
And when we go back to the sea—
whether it is to sail or to watch it—
we are going back from whence we came.

President John F. Kennedy,
toasting the America's Cup crews, September 14, 1962

The flight was fully booked,

minus the seats reserved to accommodate

sightseers do-si-doing about

the cabin.

Of the 257 dead,

114 bodies were recovered

"substantially intact";

34 were disfigured beyond recognition

until embalmers salvaged their identities

by forensic reconstruction. The remains

from 213 passengers were identified

and released to family members

and funeral directors.

Seventy-three percent of the identifications
were accomplished through dental records.
From this we can infer
a great many passengers were badly burnt
about the face.

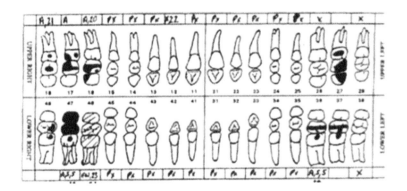

Odontograms provide
methodical, systematic charts for
tracking postmortem dental
examinations to be compared with antemortem
records, generally extensive in communities
with advanced dental care.

A hotel key
in a jacket pocket.
A fingerprint taken
and matched to an ID card
found intact due to its placement
in a hip-pocket wallet. These
were some of the clues
that helped to identify passengers.

Ultimately,
forty-four passengers were either
never positively identified or
never found.

The unidentified remains are buried,
the forty-four passengers' names engraved
at a gravesite in Waikumete Cemetery
outside Auckland.

Back to the body. The imperatives that bear
upon postmortem identification are legal,

religious, financial, social and cultural.
And if we are to honor

the dead—indeed, if we are to
remember

the dead—mustn't we confirm
and affirm their identity?

identity: *individuality; identification or the*
                     result of it; absolute sameness

                     The Australian Little Oxford
                     Dictionary, Second Edition

The pathologists declared
cause of death for everyone—

from the lady in the fur coat
to the crew and Mulgrew, who must have

been an easy ID, with his prosthetic
feet and missing fingers following

his Himalayan disaster with Hillary.
Death on flight 901 came as a result of injury

from the initial impact
and not the conflagration

that ensued after the crash,
leaving such a memorable mark

on each corpse
and the recovery team.

These harrowing injuries are referred to as
kinematic effects resulting from deceleration.

> *Deceleration: Reduction in the velocity*
> *of a moving body*

At the time of the crash, the DC-10 was traveling
around 450 mph, its three engines providing

over 50,000 pounds of thrust. The g forces
on those bodies are unimaginable

but calculable.

G: Measure of gravity acting on a body; the rate
at which gravity accelerates an object

is 1 g, or 32 feet per second squared
or 9.8 meters per second squared.

Acceleration: Technically any change in velocity
(increasing or decreasing speed).

Math time. The deceleration formula
is simple math expressed in meters squared.

$$a = \frac{v^2 - u^2}{2s}$$

a = deceleration
v = final velocity
u = initial velocity
s = distance covered

**To determine g force, find the force (measured in newtons) by
multiplying mass and acceleration. Convert total newtons to g
force by dividing total newtons by the number of newtons of
body/object equal to 1 g.**

The forces brought to bear
had such devastating kinematic effects

that among all the reports it's difficult
at times to determine

whether "extensive fragmentation" refers to
the butchered aircraft or

the destruction of the human body.
It often refers to both.

At 50-100 g's, the heart twists free
of its aortic cables. Aside from the body

colliding with objects in the cabin
(movie cameras, Champagne bottles, coffee table

books on Antarctica), the undercarriage lancing
through the seating area or any number of violent

occurrences, kinematic effects of deceleration may see
the body's long bones bend, the mesentery

and bowel tear from the abdominal
wall, soft-tissue organs

rupture. Even the cranial vault cracks. I can't help
hearing winter's skating pond split. Flailing alone

can cause limb amputation. A force higher than 350 g's
will result in total body fragmentation. This was Erebus.

A sneeze registers about 3 g's. Princess Diana's fatal injuries,
70 to 100 g's. The average body can absorb

35 g's, which is what Diana might have experienced,
experts say, had she been belted in. It's conjecture.

For the Erebus travelers, lethality comes in a snap,
less than 0.5 seconds. That's a kind of blessing.

Coroners (sic) inquest files are restricted for 50 years from year of registration on the grounds of personal privacy (including those documents in sealed envelopes). Permission to access these files must be obtained from the Coronial Services.

Item number R11888157. Your inquest
record number is the full extent

of information available to me.
R11888157 is the convincing document—

not the erroneous newspaper article or internet
memorial passenger lists (and these

are numerous)—that gets through
to me: You're dead. Cast iron

dead. "R11888157 Kay Marion Barnick."
A license to believe, the incontrovertible

document, issued
under the aegis of the Her Majesty the Queen,

R11888157 is all I have to hold
onto. I crave everything, anything,

Let no one live in oblivion

one measly coroner's
notation about you. Am I gruesome?

I've had enough fraudulence,
trailing each hearse in a limo

with frumpy window skirts.
Kay, I am not afraid to see you.

I used to be afraid
you were lost forever, you were

among those never found, fifty thousand
leagues down the envelope

of crevasse ice, in time swept out
to the salted sea. But you are among those

identified. I don't know which
is more sad. To be flung far

from the awful carcass or retrieved,
painstakingly identified after the incineration.

Many bodies were returned to families
in caskets sealed with tight screws and instructions to

never unbolt the containers. Haven't I
already looked at you?

Whatever remained of your body they "repatriated,"
shipped in the hold like a thoroughbred or Vermeer

across the International Date Line
to your home state of California,

land of the artichoke, walnut, the redwood
giant. Yet your life having been taken

at Erebus, so you also remain
at Erebus. Its steamy greeting, that laundry line

sign of life, hails mourners who to their constant
surprise don't rail at the living

volcano but bow
at the harrowing beauty that drew you here.

Let them have Antarctica. I can't
bear to remember my own happiness

anymore. My losses are far
easier to take.

Families are sworn to secrecy. Rumor

sets the average payout at US$82,000,

the longest-lived worth the least—$20K.

In 1977, by comparison, KLM compensated families

of the Tenerife crash $58,000-$600,000.

Thirty years after Erebus, Air New Zealand

refuses to confirm or deny the figures. The critical

cockpit voice recorder, under seal until 2049, could

clear up crucial transcription discrepancies

using advanced filtering technology. The tape,

however, was recently discovered

missing from the New Zealand Archives.

Marion's flying friends wasted no time
securing her legacy with a memorial scholarship.

Throughout New Zealand the Antarctic
adventurers are regularly commemorated—memorials

visited, books published, rants blogged, kids' internet
quizzes posted, plaques and artwork dedicated,

a cherry tree demurely fluttering
petals over the unidentified grave. How do I remember

Kay? Pretty soon I'll remember her
only by Erebus, by all this darkness,

though my body wants to remember
something else, the tidal pull when I was not alone.

"Never Forget" vow the old Jews
with their yahrzeits and veils.

A cashier's flabby bicep
pink as an Easter ham reveals

the smudge
of ink: "In Loving Memory, Julio."

I want to recognize
her loss but am caught

between what's private
and what's not. The black

 "You Are Not Forgotten
POW-MIA" flag cracks and tatters in town.

"Never Again 9/11" pledge countless
rear window decals

which I find this time of year
the strangest commemoration—motorized

memorials: Explorer,
Suburban, Navigator,

Armada and Avalanche
sporting Walmart reindeer antlers.

Erebus families mourned with their hands
tied behind their back

for thirty years, more, the inquiry
into the cause of the crash

transparent the way
the whiteout was.

"I found Captain Collins' ring binder diary, which I read. It contained what appeared to me to be handwritten briefing notes so I handed it to Sergeant Gilpin. It was later produced empty at the enquiry. It has never been adequately explained to me how this happened."

"What has really troubled me over the years as a police officer is the issue of pilot Captain Jim Collins' ring binder notebook, which was located amongst the wreckage and handed to me on the site. It was intact and contained numerous pages of legible technical writing and figures that indicated they related to the flying of aircraft. We recognised that this could be of importance to any investigation into the crash, and I sealed and secured it in a bag before it was returned to McMurdo. The ring binder was later produced in 1981 at the Commission of Inquiry into the disaster in an altered condition to how it was found, in that the pages were missing. It had earlier been returned to Mrs. Collins in this condition by an airline official. The reason why and how the pages came to be missing has never been satisfactorily explained or resolved."

At the thirtieth crash
anniversary, six family members

are flown down
to the mountain

for closure, that
hook and eye.

By choosing only six, by lottery, Air New Zealand
leaves hundreds remaining hurt

again, left
out, again. (Chagrined

the airline will carry many more,
104 to be exact, to Scott Base for more

ceremony.) An alb and purple stole
over a survival parka and snow

boots announce the priest, and Antarctica
is pierced anew,

one stainless steel crucifix near Erebus
and at Scott Base a 57 lb. aluminum

koru, the Maori symbol of rebirth
and return. Oh,

the stories we tell
ourselves, the catechism and prayer,

the narrative, the koru full as a cookie jar
with notes for the dead. Jam this

in too despite none of us
having any proof

our dead remember how
to read. Then why

our psalms and requiems, why in our desperate hour
do we talk to people who are nowhere

to be seen?

New Zealanders pronounce both
Cs in *Antarctica,* and after hearing it so often,

Ant•arC•ti•ca

in my search for you I'm caught
between two worlds. I think you are too.

Ritual, take this bone
from my throat. Tabernacle

monument, turbofan
engine, boot us off mountains of ice, exhaust

the hell out of emptiness. That memorial
will do. Deliver me

from the glacial landslide of loss
that never spooked you, who

loved the earth
with such devotion you dared enter her

forbidden room.

Why did it take this long
for me to realize

the airline I blindly
promoted in 1990

$$\begin{array}{r} 2012 \\ -1990 \\ \hline 22 \end{array}$$

was the airline whose numerous blunders
made this your final flight?

$$\begin{array}{r} 1990 \\ -1979 \\ \hline 11 \end{array}$$

Why didn't I understand my dream
that year in Sydney, clues

lined up neat as taxied aircraft?
How close to you

I might have come, sleuthed
vehicles that carried you, a hotel

where you'd shed
something of yourself, shaken

the hand of a pathologist
who swept the hair

from your face, tramped
the Milford Track to find

a kerchief or pithy tale
left behind. The trail is cold now.

I must have been too afraid
of not finding you. I haven't even a photo

of you—I guess it's one less item to lose. Here's a vintage
snapshot of your mother—take it,

for old time's sake. The light aircraft,
Wilco the duck, the woman: the threesome,

Wilco: Aviator shorthand
for "will comply"

an ode to flight. Why was it
so hard to lose you?

Is bringing you back
any easier?

Don't   be   afraid   of

who   you   are

Make   the   worst

of   what   you've   done

luminous

Let   no   one   live

in   oblivion

They say JFK Jr.'s corpse was dredged
from the rocky sea bottom

along with his wife's and her sister's,
quickly cremated and buried

at sea. The body! Such a drive to
recover the body, that outgrown shoe.

Japan knuckled New Zealand
to bring their 24 nationals home.

Let no one live in oblivion

So the New Zealanders prepared for Antarctica
though some on the team had never before seen

snow, and debate cranked up,
continuing today, over how dare they

risk the living
to retrieve what remained

of the dead.

Some say no one
suffered more
than the recovery
team.
David Armstrong, then an air dispatch
warrant officer in the Australian army
who unloaded aircraft in Antarctica,
spent two weeks unloading bodies.
Armstrong developed a lifelong tremor
as a result of the task.

New Zealand's police commissioner
had only recently created the Disaster

Victim Identification team
in the wake of Australia's

1977 Granville rail tragedy.
Eighty-three passengers died

when a commuter train derailed
causing a concrete and steel bridge to collapse

on top of the railroad cars. Some
died instantly, playing cards

and newspapers in hand. Others, trapped
through the night under slabs of roadway, conversed

pleasantly with rescuers for hours
only to die of crush syndrome[2]

within minutes after the weight pinning them
was finally hoisted off.

---

2 When the body experiences compression over time, cells break
down and begin to leak potassium and myoglobin, as well as other
toxic substances, into the surrounding tissues. Once the compressing
weight is removed, blood flow resumes, allowing the toxic cell
contents to spread throughout the body. A victim who was moments
ago lucid may quickly deteriorate and suffer cardiac arrhythmias
or cardiac arrest, shock, renal failure, and other organ failures. The
experience gained from accidents such as the Granville train wreck
has changed procedures for rescue operations worldwide.

FINAL APPROACH

RHV/REID-HILLVIEW

RUNWAY 13L	
Dimensions:	3100 x 75 ft./ 945 x 23 m
Surface:	asphalt, in good condition
Weight bearing capacity:	single wheel: 17.0
Runway edge lights:	medium intensity
Latitude:	37-20.190822N
Longitude:	121-49.356103W
Elevation:	123.6 ft.
Gradient:	0.4%
Traffic pattern:	left
Runway heading:	127 magnetic, 143 true
Displaced threshold:	499 ft.
Markings:	basic, in fair condition
Visual slope indicator:	2-box VASI on left (4.00 degrees glide path)
Runway end identifier lights:	yes
Touchdown point:	yes, no lights
Obstructions:	47 ft. tree, 920 ft. from runway, 205 ft. left of centerline

Kay's family buried her
nine-year-old sister

after a shop accident
at the airport her parents

owned. No prayer on earth
could hold Carol Jo to the world

of milkshakes, lilacs, those who fly
the blue skies. Two years later

Marion at her thirtieth high school reunion
in Parma, Idaho, won

two prizes: one for traveling
the farthest, one for changing

the least. How in the world
could Marion have suffered such

a loss and not have been
bruised beyond recognition? I know

how: The world's an illusion.
Not in Marion's Christian Science

sense, but in the terrible way
that allows us to misread friends. Kay spoke

neither of losing
Carol Jo nor her father so soon

after, but kept up
the extracurriculars, high school's helpful

clubs and committees, her beer can bouffant and hygiene. Why
am I hearing about this disaster

only now? I should've known
what questions to ask a friend.

And listen,

I'm afraid, is all
I did for Kay.

I have no idea and no opinion
whether Carol Jo clutched rough

white ambulance sheets or
a cold cement floor

in her last earthly grip. I'm astonished
to find my mind

imagining
if she had lived, Carol Jo

might have gone
to Antarctica instead

of Kay, and would I have been
a good friend

under those circumstances
considering the desolation

Kay must have felt
inside against the shadow

of her sister's weird news in the dark
shop? In the hour of my own dark shop I'm afraid

Kay knew the loneliness
of popular girls and the prophets

and didn't I
let her?

CMH/PORT COLUMBUS INTERNATIONAL

RUNWAY 10R	
Dimensions:	10125 x 150 ft. / 3086 x 46 m
Surface:	asphalt, in good condition
Weight bearing capacity:	single wheel: 100.0; double wheel: 200.0; double tandem: 325.0
Runway edge lights:	high intensity
Latitude:	39-59.734173N
Longitude:	082-54.536417W
Elevation:	802.9 ft.
Gradient:	0.1%
Markings:	Precision instrument, Good condition
VASI:	4-Light PAPI on Right Side of Runway
Traffic pattern:	left
Runway heading:	099 magnetic, 094 true
Runway end identifier lights:	yes
Touchdown point:	yes, no lights

My father, dragging through the loneliness
of being ninety, is perplexed

that no one dresses for air travel
anymore. In 1966 I wore an ecru Nehru jacket

on a prop flight out of Idlewild.
The stewardess pinned wings on

my brother and me
and passed a crystal bowl full

of Chiclets through the cabin
while in Columbus my grandparents

on the tarmac held down their
soft hats, awaiting our arrival.

AKL/AUCKLAND

RUNWAY 05R	
Dimensions:	11926 x 148 ft / 3635.0 x 45.1 m
Surface:	concrete
Longitude:	174.767081 / E 174° 46' 01.49"
Latitude:	-37.017303 / S 37° 01' 02.29"
End Elevation:	15.0 ft
Slope:	0.1
Alignment:	051.0
Touchdown Zone Elevation	15.0
Displaced Threshold:	1132 ft
Lighting System 1:	Centerline Lighting System
Lighting System 2:	High Intensity Runway Lights
Lighting System 3:	Runway End Identifier Lights
Lighting System 4:	Centerline and Bar
Lighting System 5:	PAPI Precision Approach Path Indicator

Awaiting the arrival of the phantom
airliner, reporters documented the eerie night

with rumors of Christchurch residents
keeping outdoor lights burning

while they slept as beacons
to help guide a crippled

jet home. I listened to the radio archives,
one broadcaster noting the absence

of pandemonium or demands

for information at the ticket counter.

"No emotional scenes, no weeping."
A sergeant guarded the family

waiting area, a priest arrived and the curtain of darkness
closed tight as a Roman collar

around them. *"Common killected,"* the Kiwi
journalist crackled into my headphones. "Waiting

for word, friends and families remain
common killected." During troubles I too

appear calm and collected. Like a sniper
in the camouflage of hope.

NZWP/WHENUAPAI-RNZAF BASE AUCKLAND

RUNWAY 03	
Dimensions:	6665 x 148 ft / 2031.5 x 45.1 m
Surface:	Asphalt, asphaltic concrete, tarmacadam, or bitumen bound macadam
Longitude:	174.620889 / E 174° 37' 15.20"
Latitude:	-36.796167 / S 36° 47' 46.20"
End Elevation:	100.0 ft
Slope:	-0.6
Touchdown Zone Elevation	Unknown
Lighting System 1:	High Intensity Runway Lights
Lighting System 2:	Center Row
Lighting System 3:	T-VASI - T-Visual Approach Slope Indicator

God, camouflaged as 80-knot headwinds,
held the dead to the Pole a little longer,

the C-130 charnel house battling out
of McMurdo, the dead

playing dead in its belly. It was almost ten
hours before the C-130 put down

at Whenuapai, Auckland's morning
skies so United Nations blue and bright

the ether must've been HEPA-filtered.
Their belongings and their ruined bodies,

forklifted off the airship, began
thawing in the heat. This was the first

airlift off the ice on the sixth
of December. Inside clear plastic

bags, the softening flesh was removed
into ambulances

for the mortuary staging.
Along the way, one driver was forced

aside with a flat
and a busted jack.

As he waited for assistance, summer's heat
roused a stench from his cargo that grew

beyond the limits of dignity.
The dead didn't want to be remembered

this way. At the same time another ambulance
driver found a corpse had shifted

unpleasantly beside him
after being rear-ended

on Karangahape Road.

The second airlift on December eleventh—
more bodies and body fragments

(a button box
of fingers and toes

and personal possessions
for identification purposes).

This time they were more wisely
transferred in unmarked refrigerated

trucks more suitable
for frozen fish and slaughtered meat.

Outside the chain link fence at Whenuapai, apart
from the few reporters, stood

Mrs. Yasuko Goto
holding a bouquet of roadside daisies.

IF THIS IS NOT YOUR FINAL DESTINATION

Religion and racing cars
I always thought good

for socking immutables in the jaw,
successes at transfiguring

the anvil on the big
toe, death's dropped anchor.

Flight could be added
to that roster. Flying,

her friends agree, was Marion's
life, and she taught it

to Kay's brother, the only family
survivor. Captain Barnick, as her son

and student became, a commercial airline pilot,
was one among scores of others

Marion put into the skies. I think of them
as apostles of flight. Maybe

he brought my friends safely
somewhere, maybe me.

And maybe Kay
didn't want to go

to the Pole after all,
and maybe she did,

but there she went, eyes wide,
ready to rake everything

in under her fingernails—the exuberance
about her! You couldn't help but hold

onto her skirts and bound along, and no one
ever had this

kindness I'm telling you about.

If I said I'll never forget her
scent, her good teeth, I've completely

forgotten.

How surprised I was to find
such good people have so many

stones to carry. Marion's
Mrs. Eddy proclaimed God,

like an Impressionist master, would never
create such a grotesque—

but even she's green gilled
and in her silk skirts, a calamity of stones.

I've seen what happens
when thirty-four years are raised

like Granville rubble.

Kay, an adventurer's daughter,
could call a Mayday

O no not I

from an early age while I was afraid
not of drowning but of calling for help.

Let no one live in oblivion

My pulse gets ahead of itself
every time I read the lie

of early rescuers finding footprints
leading away from the crash, no more

a deception than saying
I never forgot, not

for one minute. For years
and years I forgot! The truth is

I didn't come here for you. It's you
who's come for me—

in my dreams, softly in spruce forests . . .
rustling in the backseat of my car . . . under

the counter in coffee shops, my hand held.
You're with me at this moment.

Thirty-five-year-old Norwegian
Aleksander Gamme films himself in 2011 trekking

to the South Pole and back. Lightening his pack,
Gamme buries supplies in the ice

at various waypoints.

On Day 86 of his three-month venture,

Gamme digs out a stash of provisions. The camera captures
screams of unrestrained joy at his finding

two bags of Cheez Doodles.
Then, pausing in stunned Antarctic silence,

Gamme wonders, *Is this real?*
I'm going crazy! Gamme has no memory

of packing the Cheez Doodles.
What was forgotten

won't impair his enjoyment of
what lies before him. Quite the opposite.

Take this
coat, the umbrella. We can walk together

again. You aren't fearful of living
in oblivion. We're the ones fearful

of forgetting,
our memorials, our monuments speak

to this dread. Now
the day approaches

when I'll wake to look
so much like you. I think I'm beginning to.

When you say the water's rising
it's not figurative.

Antarctica's massive ice shelves are shrinking
because they are being eaten away from below
by warm water, a new study finds.
That suggests that future sea levels
could rise faster
than many scientists have been predicting.

Daily Mail, *25 April 2012*

The tide ferries those
we know and those unknown

down mapped waterways. Sooner or later everyone goes
home, wherever that is. You seemed

always at home, or I was
in you

when we met and I was sick of
telling lies about myself. Now I'm sick

of telling the truth. Maybe that's why
everything makes me cry, Kay—

the Antarctic fairground
animals' fate,

the water that keeps rising,
talk of the heat

above and below,
the collapse of ice,

global instability.
I thought I'd given up

my search for higher ground
but here you are,

Kay Barnick,
from the netherworld

light into New York's illustrated
night, and you love me.

AFTERWORD

Following the disaster, Air New Zealand's Antarctic sightseeing flights immediately ceased, its CEO resigned and the fleet underwent a complete redesign. Photographs of the sooty remnants, particularly of the tail with its familiar koru logo, became indelible images in the minds of New Zealanders.

In 2012 Air New Zealand was awarded Airline of the Year Award by the leading industry magazine, its second win of the decade. The airline was particularly noted for "setting the standards for aircraft, environment and operational performance."

An Australian company, Antarctica Sightseeing Flights, has been flying private charter tourists from Melbourne over the Pole since 1994 (avoiding the area around Mt. Erebus) but no one had been offering such trips out of New Zealand since the Erebus crash. In 2011 the Australian airline decided to offer its first flights from New Zealand to Antarctica. The company canceled its Auckland program in February 2012 when its 747 failed to book more than 30% of available seats. Potential passengers were refunded in full and given a discount toward the purchase of tickets departing Australia for the Pole. According to its website, the company flies its 747s out of five Australian cities to this "pristine wilderness," at "approximately 10,000 feet above sea level, which brings us within 2,000 feet off the highest point."

TE901 PASSENGERS AND CREW

ADDIS, Peter James
AISENMAN, Lleone Margaret
ALLAN, Alan Lawrence Malyon
ALLAN, Jane Phillipa
ALLAN, Marjorie Townley
ANDERSON, Audrey Gordon
ANDERSON, Margret Isabel
ANGLESEY, Grant William
ARMITAGE, Ethel Mary
ARNOLD, Melinda Maria
ARNOLD, Valerie Ellen
ASHTON, Graham Mitford
BAGNALL, Mr.
BAGNALL, Mrs.
BAINBRIDGE, Thomas Eric
BALDWIN, Llewellyn Arnold (Peter)
BARNICK, Kay Marion
BARNICK, Marion Ruth
BEAUMONT, Earl Aubrey
BECKETT, Desmond William
BLAIR, Patricia Adele
BOND, Marilyn Alma
BOND, Robin Melville
BREHAUT, Ronald Thomas
BROAD, Jon Philip Dr
BROAD, Philippa Margaret
BROOKS, Geraldine Kay
BROUGH, Aubrey Conroy
BUCHANAN, Geoffrey
BURCKHALTER, Lucille Clark
BURGESS, Lindsay Robert
BURGESS, Rose Ellen
BURGI, Heinz
BURTON, Lorraine Eileen
BUTLER, Rae Jeanne

CAMERON, Rangiaho
CAMPBELL, Stuart Donald
CARLETON, John Barrie
CARLETON, Marion Rennie
CARR, Margaret Bell
CHADDERTON, Brian Harry
CHADDERTON, Valerie Enid
CHRISTIANSEN, Alla
CHRISTMAS, Hugh Francis
CLARK, David
CLARK, Irene Alice
CLARK, Iris
CLARK, William Henry
COCKRILL, Joan Audrey
COLBRAN, Cyril Bernard
COLBRAN, Yvonne Louise
COLE, John Wright
COPAS, Jean Ann Barnett
COPLEY, Susan Elaine
COPSEY, Audrey Joy
COREY, Constance Dr
CRABTREE, Mary Alison
CRABTREE, Norman David
DAHL, Marie Patricia
DAVIES, June
DAWSON, Peter Massie
DEAN, Kay
DEBBAGE, Florence Daisy
DEMAGE, Nora Violet
DUFF, Helen Dora
DUKE, Athol David
DYKZUEL, Hermanus Adrianus Johannes Maria Douglas
DYKZUEL, Johannes Cabrini Maria
EAGLES, Gwen Louise
EDWARDS, Edna Miriam
EDWARDS, Elizabeth Jane
EMMETT, Cecillia Campbell
EMMETT, John Barnham

FERRELL, Jean
FROST, Katherine Edith Janet
FURUKAWA, Kuniyasu
GALLAGHER, Alfred James
GALLAGHER, Elsie Thelma
GIBBS, Brucie
GILLIVER, Richard
GOSLING, Violet Iris
GOTO, Norio
GULLAND, Pamela Margaret
HANCE, Florence Lee
HANSEN, Marlene Anne
HARRIS, Hazel Phoebe
HARRISON, Annie
HARRISON, Muriel Florence Rose
HARTLEY, James Follett
HARTY, Myra Pearl
HAWORTH, Kathleen
HAWORTH, Peter
HIGUCHI, Mitsuo
HILL, Eileen Elsie
HILL, Gordon Alexander
HOLLOWAY, Jean Marie
HOLTHAM, Bryan Ernest
HOTSON, Roy Henry
HOUGHTON, John Greenleaf
HOWARTH, Ralph Brenton
HUGHES, Steven William
HUMPHREY, Mildred Alice
HYNDMAN, Thomas William Noel
IMAI, Akira
IMAI, Hisao
JAHN, Ernest Adalbert
JAHN, Isabel
JARVIS, Nicholas Dunstan
JENKINS, Evelyn Lois
JENNINGS, Charles Ivory
KARL, Kathleen Florence

KEARNEY, Dennis Frances
KEITH, John Edgar
KENDON, Nancy Phyllis
KERR, Betty
KERR, Francis Ronald
KERR, Geoffrey Ian Hamilton
KILSBY, Anthony John
KILSBY, Geoffrey Michael
KING, Nancy
KIRK, Donald Clive
KITAGAWA, Asako
KLASSOVITY, Paul Anthony
KLENSCH, Carl Robert
LAKE, Mary Louise
LARSEN, William Olaf
LAVIN, James Francis
LEPINE, Yves
LIES, Michael Ralph
LING, Alison Louise
LOCHER, Urs
LOMAX, William Brian
LOUGHNAN, Charles Henry Devenish
LOUGHNAN, Patrick Louis
MacKENZIE, John Alexander
MacKENZIE, Margaret Joyce (Peg)
MacKENZIE, Stella Vonomerie
MADGWICK, Eudora Emily
MAGNELL, Muriel
MAGNELL, Theodore James
MANLEY, David Victor
MANN, Dorothy Maude
MARSDEN, Dorothy
MARSDEN, Joseph Alan
MARTIN, Sarah Jane
MASKELYNE, Trevor John
MASON, Robert
MATTHEWS, Barbara Dawn
MAYNARD, Olive Myrtle

MAYNARD, William George
McDONALD, Shirley Jane
McKENDRY, Richard John
McMILLIAN, John Bruce
McMILLIAN, Melba Pearl
McNAMARA, Bernard Joseph
McNEIL, Eric Albert Dunbar
MEIER, Jurg
MITCHELL, Mark Geoffrey
MITSUHASHI, Junichi
MITSUHASHI, Nakako
MUNRO, Ross
MURRAY, Owen John
NICHOLSON, Christine Margaret
NODA, Shigeru
O'CONNOR, Ian John
ODANI, Hiroko
ODANI, Morihiko
OLIVER, Mervyn John
ONO, Tetsuro
OSAWA, Juhei
OSAWA, Masa
OZAWA, Norio
PALMER, David Lloyd
PALMER, Edward James
PALMER, Gary Kent
PARKKARI, Eija Kylli Marjatta
PATERSON, Ethel Mary
PATERSON, Linda Jan
PAYKEL, Nola Minchin
PAYNE, Alfred Murray
PEACOCKE, Majorie Ethel Isabella
PETHERS, Carla
PLUMMER, Alexander Francis
PLUMMER, Hilda Francis
POTTER, Michael Arthur Edwin
PRESTON, Robert John
PRICE, Beatrice Irene

PRICE, Beverley
PRIDMORE, Joy Anges
RAWLINS, Valerie (Vere) Mary
REVELL, Basil Halvor
REVELL, Eileen Geraldine
RICHMOND, Pamela Gayl
ROBB, Helen Lady
ROBERTS, Alison Meryl
ROBERTS, Michael Seaver
ROBINSON, Betty Estelle
RUDEN, Karl
SATO, Hisako
SCOTT, Marie Theresa
SEKI, Michi
SEKI, Toshiro
SHEPPARD, George M
SHIGETA, Seishrio
SHINONOYA, Ryoichi
SMITH, Betty Louise
SMYTHE, Henry Howard
STEEL, Ralph Augustus
STEVENSON, Anthony James Leonard
STEWART, Donald Matthew
STOKES, Alan Maxwell
STOREY, Phyllis May
TAKADA, Masaaki
TANTON, Peter Alex
TAYLOR, Douglas Clement Frank
THOMAS, Roy Pearce
THOMAS, Walter Daniel
THOMPSON, Billie Tadlock
THOMPSON, Henry Ford
THOMPSON, Watson
TREMAINE, Florence Anne
TREMAINE, Robert David
TRINDER, Elaine Frances
WARD, Henry
WARD, Valerie

WATSON, Isobel
WATSON, Katherine
WEBB, Alfred William
WILLIAMS, Janet Challis
WILLIAMS, Janet Mary
WILLIAMS, Leonard Heathcote
WOOD, Barbara Annie
WOOD, Irvine Kirkham
WORTH, Linda
YANAGISAWA, Hamako
YANAGISAWA, Nobuyoshi
YOKOYAMA, Ryoji
ZOLL, Otmar

COLLINS Thomas James *Captain*
CASSIN Gregory Mark *First Officer*
LUCAS Graham Neville *First Officer*
BROOKS Gordon Barrett *Flight Engineer*
MOLONEY Nicholas John *Flight Engineer*
BENNETT David John Senior *Assistant Purser*
CARR-SMITH Elizabeth Mary *Cabin Crew*
CATER Graham Ronald *Senior Cabin Crew*
COLLINS Martin John *Purser*
FINLAY Michael James *Assistant Purser*
KEENAN Dianne *Assistant Cabin Crew*
LEWIS James Charles *Assistant Cabin Crew*
MARINOVIC Suzanne Margaret *Senior Cabin Crew*
MAXWELL Bruce Rhodes *Cabin Crew*
MORRISON Katrina Mary *Cabin Crew*
McPHERSON Roy William *Chief Purser*
MULGREW Peter *In-flight Commentator*
SCOTT Russell Morrison *Purser*
SICKLEMORE David Brian *Cabin Crew*
SIMMONS Stephen George *Cabin Crew*
WOLFERT Marie-Therese *Cabin Crew*

EREBUS

NOTES

p. 19   The Queen's Birthday is an annual public holiday in most of the British Commonwealth, celebrated the first Monday in June in New Zealand, though Elizabeth II was born 21 April 1926.

p. 35   "Not Jehovah's Witness . . ." Marion Barnick was a devout Christian Scientist. (See note below, *Champagne breakfast*).

p. 39   *Ninety-Nines* An international organization of women pilots, started in 1929 and named for its ninety-nine charter members. (Amelia Earhart was its first president.) In the end, the group decided not to take the Antarctic flight—all except for Jean Ferrell (a flight instructor for United Airlines and the trip organizer), along with Marion and Kay. Jean Ferrell's name is engraved on the mass memorial for those whose bodies were never recovered or whose remains were never identified.

p. 40   *Champagne breakfast* Marion, in accordance with her religion, didn't drink. This didn't mean she had no sense of humor about it. In 1970 she and her husband, traveling extensively by small plane, were of course required to radio quite frequently. Her aircraft's registration, ending in PW, allowed Marion to remark she and her husband had "Papa Whiskeyed" across Africa.

p. 56   *170 Second Avenue* This 17-story prewar building, the site of the NY Historical Society in 1857, was always attractive but certainly nothing near the million-dollar apartments now being offered for sale. A two bedroom, one bathroom, recently sold for over $2,200,000.

p. 56   *Binibon* Open all night and cheap, this tiny East Village dive, where my brother and I might share a dish of Chicken LaMama (chicken stewed with raisins, cinnamon, apple, soy and sesame oil) and brown rice, closed shortly after Norman Mailer's protégé, Jack Abbot, fatally knifed a young waiter in 1981.

p. 56 *Harry Kondoleon, Tony Holland, John Duka* Harry Kondoleon, ingenious playwright, college alum and Astoria native, took a neighboring East Village apartment after Yale Drama School; through byzantine connections, brilliant, mordant Tony Holland, a hard-working actor, landed me the interview leading to the job where Kay and I met; John Duka, fashion and style writer of great wit and generous soul, worked at the company where Kay and I met before moving to the *New York Times*.

p. 66 "The fearful passage of their death-mark'd love" Shakespeare, *Romeo & Juliet,* prologue.

p. 67 This spectral image was published in Gordon Vette's book *Impact Erebus* exactly as reproduced here, the faces inelegantly cut away in pre-Photoshop days. Vette, at the time of the crash an Air New Zealand pilot, initiated his own independent investigation of the crash. Vette's *Impact Erebus* summarizes his findings, which damaged many friendships and his career, such was the contentiousness of the debate over the accident. Vette's expertise, however, was critical in the discussion and led to innovations in safety, including a forward-looking (rather than the previous ground-directed) ground proximity warning system (GPWS).

p. 91 "Bear with me; My heart is in the coffin there with Caesar, And I must pause till it come back to me." Shakespeare, *Julius Caesar,* Act III, scene 2.

p. 109 The remarks that begin this section, though unattributed here, are recollections by actual recovery team members and others, including Gregory Gilpin, Ray Goldring, Stuart Leighton, Jim Morgan, Mark Penn, and Nigel Roberts, and have been minimally edited by this writer.

p. 122 1556 陝西地震死亡近 100 萬人死亡人數最多的地震紀錄 The 1556 Shaanxi earthquake killed nearly one million people, the deadliest earthquake on record.

p. 124 *"persistent, intense and deep seated* [sic] *fire"* From the report by Chief Inspector of Air Accidents Ron Chippindale.

p. 130 Is it an irony that Eliot Porter's *Antarctica,* a popular book of photographic essays, which many of the sightseers brought with them on the flight, survived the crash intact while their owners did not?

p. 139 The Marion Barnick Memorial Scholarship for young women aviators was established in honor of Marion, a highly experienced pilot. She participated in numerous races and was a respected and adored instructor. Barnick, who began flying in 1939 and with her husband ran a flight school at the Reid-Hillview airport in San Jose, never missed an opportunity to boost the role of women in aviation, whether through formal channels or casually, chatting up folks in a coffee shop or strangers on a supermarket line.

p. 141 The first inquiry into the accident, led by chief of air accidents Ron Chippindale, found pilot error the cause of the crash. The public outcry in response to the Chippindale findings led to an inquiry headed by Justice Peter Mahon, absolving the pilots of responsibility. After this Royal Commission concluded its hearings into the air disaster, an Air New Zealand employee came forward to admit he removed the pages of the pilot's notebook because they contained no information pertaining to the flight and were soaked in kerosene. The two police officers who found and took possession of the binder at the site of the crash contested that assertion. In fact, many believe the notebook contained the coordinates given at Captain Collins' 9 November 1979 briefing along with authorization to descend to altitudes given by McMurdo Air Traffic Control.

SOURCES

Air Transport World online: http://atwonline.com/videos/atws-2012-airline-year-air-new-zealand-0221

Antarctica Sightseeing Flights: www.antarcticaflights.com.au/

Army News, Issue 428, February 2012, www.army.mil.nz

British Dental Journal, April 2001, Volume 190 No 7, pp. 359-366

Cullen, S.A., M.D. FRCPath. "Injuries in Fatal Aircraft Accidents." ftp.rta.nato.int/public//PubFullText/...///EN-HFM-113-03.pdf Paper presented at the RTO HFM Lecture Series on "Pathological Aspects and Associated Biodynamics in Aircraft Accident Investigation," held in Madrid, Spain, 28-29 October 2004; Königsbrück, Germany, 2-3 November 2004, and published in RTO-EN-HFM-113.

The Erebus Story: http://www.erebus.co.nz/

Foghorn, January 11, 2010 (Newsletter of the Ninety-Nines, Inc., Bay Cities chapter), http://baycities99.org

Mahon, Peter. *Verdict on Erebus.* Auckland: Collins, 1984

New Zealand Airline Pilots Association: http://www.erebus.co.nz/

New Zealand History online: http://www.nzhistory.net.nz/

New Zealand Herald, "Erebus Crash Cash Revealed," by Jane Phare, 15 November 2009: http://www.nzherald.co.nz/mt-erebus-crash/news/article.cfm?c_id=1500932&objectid=10609328

Ross Sea Info: Geology, Glaciology and Wildlife: http://www.rosssea.info/sub-antarctic-bird-life.html

Swarbrick, Nancy. "Air crashes - The 1979 Erebus crash," Te Ara - the Encyclopedia of New Zealand, updated 2-Mar-09: URL: http://www.TeAra.govt.nz/en/air-crashes/5

Vette, Gordon. *Impact Erebus.* (Auckland: Hodder & Stoughton) 1983

Vij, Krishan. *Textbook of Forensic Medicine and Toxicology: Principles and Practice.* New Delhi: Elsevier, 2011.

The Volunteers, Vol. 36, No. 1, p. 12, "Citation – New Zealand Special Service Medal (Erebus)," issuu.com/nzmhs/docs/nzmhs

CREDITS

Page 26
Title: Baggage Tag
Author's personal collection

Page 28
Title: International Date Line
Credit: Royal Society of New Zealand

Page 39
Title: John Gould Skua
Credit: Shapero Rare Books

Page 48, 49
Title: "Montagues and Capulets," Sergei Prokofiev
Public Domain

Page 56
Title: 170 Second Avenue
Credit: Douglas Elliman Real Estate

Page 60
Title: Ford to City: Drop Dead
Credit: *The Daily News*, October 30, 1975

Page 67
Title: Passenger Photographs, redacted
Images appeared in *Impact Erebus*, Gordon Vette (Hodder & Stoughton: Auckland), 1983

Page 71
Title: Assumed Orbiting Sequence
Credit: Report of the Royal Commission

Page 72
Title: Actual Orbiting Sequence
Credit: Report of the Royal Commission

Page 82
Title: Photograph of Impact
Image appeared in *Impact Erebus*, Gordon Vette (Hodder & Stoughton: Auckland), 1983

Page 86
Title: "Comet Smear"
Approved for use as a public document

Page 89
Title: Kathleen Scott
Photographer unknown

Page 108
Title: New Zealand mountaineers assist police recovery teams' search for bodies during aftermath of Air New Zealand DC10 crash near base of Ross Island, Antarctica.
Credit: Colin Monteath, Hedgehog House New Zealand

Page 131
Title: Odontogram
Public Domain

Page 145
Title: Marion and Wilco
Credit: *Foghorn*, January 11, 2010

ACKNOWLEDGMENTS

Sections of this manuscript appear in the anthology *Devouring the Green: Fear of a Human Planet* (Jaded Ibis Press). Thanks to Sam Witt for his remarkable editorial grafting skills, and to my tireless agent Malaga Baldi, who searches to find me a place in the world.

I have the best publisher, bar none. Seth Pennington, who proofed and copyedited the manuscript with an understanding of the interactions of form and content, kept the book clean, clear, and comprehensible. There is nothing Associate Editor Sarah Rawlinson can't do, and if she felt exasperated by me she never was the least bit testy over my nagging questions. Publisher Bryan Borland totally understood the book from our first conversation. A better husband the book could never find.

Gay Bryant and Julia Zaetta, two magazine editors of incomparable vision, imagination and courage partnered to send me to Australia in 1990 in a life-altering job exchange. That experience, significant in and of itself, profoundly influenced my access to this work. I'm indebted to both women.

Members of That Creative Thing—Sandra García-Betancourt, Mallika Dutt, Idelisse Malavé, Sara Mejia Kriendler, Agunda Okeyo, Jacqui Starkey, Joanne Sandler—an alliance of artists, continue to pull me out of the ebb tide.

Elizabeth Coit, Amy Finsilver, Greg Gottlieb, KC Hartman, and Andrea Parks supported me with intermittent labor or outright gifts while I was at work on this project. I am deeply grateful for their unstinting generosity.

Every writer puts her friends through the grind of manuscript reading. I am so lucky to have such friends as Cooper Blumenthal, Bara Levin, Joanne Sandler, Maggie Stern Terris, and, especially, Megan Taylor, who read countless versions.

This work is the result of my MFA thesis at Goddard College. During my four residencies on the Vermont campus, the faculty acted as hothouse for this book. My advisors Elena Georgiou and Jan Clausen imparted their Promethean knowledge, uncomplainingly scrutinizing revision after revision. Theirs was a gargantuan effort. Any remaining flaws are only a reflection of my own limitations. My far-flung friends in the low-residency graduate program were the audience who answered the writer's eternal question, What's the point? They are loved.

More research was required for this book than for any single work I'd previously written. The following people have been indispensable to this effort:

Verna West, my missing link! A friend of Marion Barnick's through the 99s, Ms. West provided me with scores of photographs and in-depth background information. Without her, this story would not have gotten off the ground.

Tanvi Karnik and Mohini Shroff of the Indian Woman Pilots Association so willingly shared their memories of Marion Barnick, Shroff's mentor.

Shroff described Marion as "gracious beyond imagination." I might say the same of every New Zealander who participated in this project. Jill Mellanby of the Royal Society of New Zealand allowed reprint rights with a goodwill and benevolence that surprised this native New Yorker. All New Zealand interactions followed in the same charitable vein. Mark Leevers, Duty Officer, Coastguard Northern Region, NZ, provided information recalled from his classroom viewing of crash-scene evidence. Vanessa Tedesco of Christchurch City Libraries along with its LiveOnline Fingertip Librarian spent unstinting hours helping research the provenance of images. Chris Adams, New Zealand Air Line Pilots' Association, assisted as liaison in contacting retired government workers. I extend my deepest gratitude to everyone involved in Operation Overdue, particularly the photographers and diarists from the body recovery team who so kindly allowed me to excerpt and adapt their harrowing words for this work: Gregory Gilpin, Ray Goldring, Stuart Leighton, Colin Monteath, Jim Morgan, Mark Penn, and Nigel Roberts. It could not have been a benign experience for them to grant us permission to publish, even after all these years, let alone to edit, however slightly, their words and photos. Theirs was a gesture of remarkable grace.

My beloved family (some of whom are resolute in thinking writing is highly interruptible work) supplied me with *agedashi dofu* and a room of my own in various locations, including occasionally at the massively inspirational XV Beacon Hotel in Boston, in which I could "let the line of thought dip deep into the stream." They may not all be as understanding as Virginia Woolf but they accept that this is what I do, it can't be helped. Their inimitable humor and sharing of dog company were of enormous assistance. Thank you all.

Finally, all my dentists and doctors, particularly Joanne Ahola, Sharon B. Diamond, Diane E. Meier, and Ralph Neaderland (in memoriam), who have been so kind to the body I came here with—my gratitude is immeasurable.

ABOUT THE AUTHOR

After two decades editing women's magazines and more than ten years in geriatrics as a cultural arts specialist, Ms. Summer recently found equilibrium working as a jack-of-all-trades, which safeguards time for writing. Her short stories and poetry have appeared in *Ploughshares, Spoon River Poetry Review, Literal Latte, Oregon East*, and other publications and anthologies. Her novel *The Silk Road* (2000), recently recorded for Audible. com, was nominated for numerous prizes. *Not the Only One* (2004), an anthology of stories for gay adolescents edited by Ms. Summer, was recognized by the New York Public Library as one of the year's best books for teens. A.M. Homes selected Ms. Summer's story "Peaceful Village" for inclusion in the 2013 edition of *The Masters Review.* She's most charmed by her 1998 essay on memorable meals winning an award from Ruth Reichl in a *New York Times'* food-writing contest. Ms. Summer is a Kirkland College graduate with an MFA from Goddard College. A third-generation New Yorker, she dreams regularly of those who've gone before her.

ABOUT THE PRESS

Sibling Rivalry Press is an independent publishing house based in Little Rock, Arkansas. Our mission is to publish work that disturbs and enraptures. www.siblingrivalrypress.com

GRATITUDE

This book was produced, in part, due to the support of the non-profit Sibling Rivalry Press Foundation. The Sibling Rivalry Press Foundation supports small presses and small press authors through grants and fiscal sponsorship. For more about the Sibling Rivalry Press Foundation, visit www.srpfoundation.org.

CPSIA information can be obtained at www.ICGtesting.com
Printed in the USA
LVOW05s1517100215

426287LV00006B/5/P